Cashing Out

A handbook for selling your creative services company,
and a million reasons not to do it

By Jon Kolko

Copyright & Use

Narrative

Disclaimer

The author is not a lawyer, and this should not be considered legal advice. The author is also not a CPA or tax professional, and this should not be considered financial advice. Nothing in this book constitutes legal, tax, accounting, investment or other professional advice. You should seek appropriate counsel for your own situation. The content is for information purposes only; the author makes no representations as to the accuracy or completeness of any information in this book. The author will not be liable for any errors or omissions in this information and will not be liable for any losses, injuries, or damages from the use of this information.

To my wife Jess, who helped me through the anxiety and stress of selling my company, and to my Co-Founders Matt Franks and Chad Fisher; thank you for creating something great with me.

Contents

Introduction

In 2017, my partners and I founded a design strategy company called Modernist Studio. We grew the revenue and headcount, and in the peak of our growth—in August, of 2021—we sold the company. I had no idea what I was doing, and I constantly felt like I was doing it wrong. There are only a few playbooks for how to sell a company, and the resources I *could* find focused on selling a software startup, not a design or strategy services company. Even after spending time with founders and mentors whom I was lucky enough to have personal relationships with, I still felt like I was flying blind, and in retrospect, I made all sorts of errors. I wished there were examples and case studies I could learn from that were specifically about creative services companies.

This book—primarily made up of a series of interviews with founders who have sold design and strategy consultancies—is the set of conversations that I wish I could have read prior to selling my own company. You'll hear from people who built companies from scratch, who navigated complex financial processes, who negotiated (some better, and some worse), and who exited their services companies a little richer and a lot wiser.

Throughout the book, I've interspersed more pragmatics about what to expect during the acquisition process—things related to the process, negotiations, earnouts, and so-on, that I wish I knew more about before I started my own process. And along the way, I've pulled out some themes and details that are particularly helpful in making thoughtful decisions about a sale or acquisition.

But here's the tldr (too long, didn't read) from my whole set of interviews. It's a takeaway that's so obvious and so dumb to say, but so easily missed:

When you sell your company, it's no longer yours.

As a founder and entrepreneur, you likely got to where you are now because of your tenacity, grit, and do-whatever-it-takes attitude in order to have your company succeed. These skills and qualities help control and manage the ambiguity of birthing a new thing and helping it grow and flourish. You built a *creative* business because you love to make things. You took chances, not just because building a company is a gamble, but because *creativity demands risk*. And you built a culture of people who care about *craft*, and *feelings*, and *each other*. It's your company, and your fingerprints, heart and soul are all over it.

Nearly all of the people I interviewed recalled frustration during the acquisition and post-acquisition process because the people they suddenly worked with and worked for had other priorities, other perspectives, and other opinions on what was best. Common sense says the entrepreneur should have expected this; they didn't, and neither did I in my own sale.

The differences and conflicts they encountered were all about creativity.

The founders I interviewed explained that an acquirer cares about *optimizing things*, not making things. The new owners care about *minimizing risk* through process and procedure. They've created *their own culture*, and want to maintain it. Sometimes these differences were small and easy to work through. Sometimes they were fundamental to the success of the acquisition. But for founders and design leaders, recognizing and embracing that simple point— *when you sell your company, it's no longer yours*—is critical before deciding to embark on a sale.

Creativity is one of the most important forces we have for directing positive change in the world, and the people who run design companies are often in leadership roles because they are wonderful designers. However, as many designers are often quick to point out, they may not necessarily feel equipped to be the most savvy business people. I hope that these interviews and observations can help these designer-owners make reasoned and intelligent decisions about the future of their companies as they support their teams and recognize the financial benefits of their hard work.

Before we get started, here are some quick notes about the people I interviewed:

First, I was pretty loose in my definition of a "creative design consultancy." Most of the founders and leaders I spoke with were at the helm of companies that provided a broad range of primarily digital services, like experience strategy, design research, visual and interaction design, product and app design, and so-on. I'm pretty confident these results generalize to other forms of creative services, like advertising, print design, industrial design, copywriting, and so-on, and if you're in those worlds, I would love to hear if these stories resonate with you, too.

Next, I've tried hard to include founders from a variety of cultural, socioeconomic, and ethnic backgrounds. But even with my best intentions, I struggled a great deal to find design consultancies that were started by women and then sold, and I found even fewer that were started by people of color and then sold. This speaks to a large gap in all aspects of the M&A process related to creative service companies: people who have historically been left out of the entrepreneurial process *still* are.

Additionally, this book is highly US-centric. That is less of a comment on the entrepreneurial state of the world and more about my own set of contacts—most of the people I've included here crossed paths with me at frog design in the US at some point. But in casual conversation with creative entrepreneurs from other countries, I've found that many of the situations you'll read about in these interviews are familiar, particularly related to finances, control, and a self-described naivety around business as compared to creativity.

I also want to share one final thought before we dive in. Without exception, the people I spoke with made a good amount of money on their sale. Sometimes that money was "buy a house money." Sometimes it was truly life changing, even described as "fuck you money." But nearly all of the participants were reluctant to talk about and share the specifics of the finances of the deal, not necessarily because of nondisclosure agreements, but because of *shame* that they would be judged negatively for generating this level of personal wealth. They explained (often after asking me to turn the recorder off) that they felt like they had broken some sort of sacred rule of creativity by selling their companies.

Yet we read about and constantly celebrate *product* entrepreneurs—like the founders of Instagram or PayPal—for selling their companies for millions of dollars, and in these types of sales, the finances and the founders are the centerpieces of the story.

Our industry has work to do here. We need to get over the negative "selling out" attitude and culture. If you created something great, and proudly sold it, there should never be *shame* in the financial part of the outcome. Regret? Things to do differently? Sure. But I hope that we can evolve our thinking so that creativity and money can live hand-in-hand and designers can feel satisfaction in the financial side of their efforts, too. There's nothing easy about running a creative consultancy. Cashed out? Scream it to the world, with pride—you earned it.

Maria Giudice, Who Founded Hot Studio and Sold It to Facebook in 2013

Let's start with a conversation with Maria Giudice, who founded Hot Studio, a user experience and product design company. After 20 years, Maria sold it to Facebook in what was, at the time, considered to be the largest design talent acquisition ever.

Maria, tell me a little about Hot Studio prior to the acquisition.

My whole professional career was led through people-centered design. I really leaned into design being a vehicle to help people make sense of the world and focus very religiously on what people need, want and desire in life, and really lead from that perspective.

Hot was a company that allowed us to do that work for hundreds of clients. It was full service; we offered everything from business strategy to engineering execution. It was around 80 people, located in San Francisco and New York.

It was a great culture. I really invested a lot in creating an environment where people could maximize their creativity, feel psychologically safe, and be able to be their best selves. And it was wild. It was diverse. We had 50% women, we had people of color, and it was a real safe, diverse company, where people liked to work. And we threw lots of great parties.

It was quality, above all else. We were profitable, but we weren't driven by profit. We used profit to sustain our ability to do great work. I always believe you hire people much smarter than you, who are better than you. It was no bullshit; you can't be egoless, but it wasn't driven by ego. It was driven by a desire to do your best work.

We did everything. Marketing sites, web applications... We had one of the first apps released on the iPad. We dabbled in interactive TV experiences. We worked with nonprofits. It was everything that you can imagine in the digital space.

How did the company start, and how did it grow?

When I got out of school, I was working for Richard Saul Wurman. He got a gig to redesign the Yellow Pages in California. I went there for three months, and I didn't leave. It was the dawn of the digital age for Apple; it was 1987. We were asking, "What is this computer? What's Illustrator and Photoshop? How do we use it?" And I really fell in love with the intersection of design and technology.

I started freelancing, and then I got busy. And then I hired some friends. And then I was like, "I have a company. I got a BFA. How do I do this?" And then I figured it out on the job.

Growth was slow and steady. I had just two employees working with me in '97. And then it went up to 20 in '99. And then there was the dot com bust; companies like Phoenix Pop and companies that I was already competing with disappeared overnight. I had some steady clients that just kept me alive.

It went from 20 to 15 employees for a while. In 2003 there were downturns here and there, and then from 2007 on, it was slow and steady.

We started having disciplines; we started organizing. And so once we had PM and visual design and UX and engineering, and then we scaled so we could take on the kind of projects from beginning to end that we wanted. And that's how it got to about 80.

Do you remember what payroll was for 80 people?

Yeah, I do, because it kept me up at night. It was a 1.3 million-a-month burn. We had to bring in 1.7 or 1.8 million dollars every month in order to turn a profit.

And that kept me up. We survived three major downturns. It was so mentally exhausting. When I hired somebody, I was so careful, because I knew that I was creating a contract with that person. I'm going to hire you. I'm going to support you. I'm going to support your family, and in return, you're going to do this for me. And I really took it personally with every single person who worked at Hot Studio. That was my thing. I cared about every person there.

I started getting tired. I started getting really exhausted. I had two kids. I had this large payroll. It fucked with my head when things were bad. It kept me up at night. And when I was in my mid-forties, I started telling myself, "I don't know if I want to do this anymore." I didn't know if I could handle another downturn. It felt like a hamster wheel.

People were always interested in an acquisition of Hot Studio, and I was never against it. But potential buyers just didn't get what we were doing and why we were doing it. They saw us as skills, but they didn't really pay attention to the culture and all the special stuff that we had.

I have enough people in my inner circle, like Clement Mok (who sold Studio Archetype to Sapient), Kevin Farnham (who sold Method to GlobalLogic), and Christopher Ireland (who sold Cheskin to WPP). There were a lot of people who I knew, like Simon Smith (who sold Phoenix Pop to Liquid Thinking), who went through acquisitions which just sucked. So I had a lot of models and role models. I had a lot of advice from these people: pay attention to this, don't pay attention to that.

There were also these M&A people, these hardcore white guys who I just didn't relate to—they didn't see the people-value. They were looking at EBITDA, they were looking at all the things that they are supposed to, but I didn't feel like they got the secret sauce of what Hot Studio was.

And then, Facebook approached us. They were our client, and they were basically renting our people because they didn't have enough designers. It became a conversation—"We want your people, but we don't want to steal your people." They had a bit of a soul back then!

It was December of 2012, and I was called into Facebook to talk to Sheryl and Mark. I did not know that was going to happen. I walked in, and it was Mark and Sheryl grilling me about Hot Studio and why I would want to sell my company. And I wasn't prepared, but somehow I didn't fuck it up. And then there was a negotiation for three months; I turned 50 in February, and then I sold my company in March. We sold it on March 14th, 2013: that's when we announced to the world that we sold Hot Studio.

Tell me about the process.

We signed an LOI, and then we had to share our books; anything that they asked for. And we had to agree to incredible confidentiality. The code name of the acquisition was called Hot Tamale. And it had to be done in a cloak of secrecy. I shared the news with my leadership team, all the directors, and they were interviewed. But Facebook didn't have access to interview anybody else; that was my demand. Because I didn't want it to unravel. So my directors had to basically present portfolios of every single designer, and advocate for that person.

They didn't hire everybody. They only really wanted the designers. I was so worried about legacy; I told them that it couldn't be 20 people who go, it had to be a majority. So I think the number we agreed on was like 55. They had to hit a number to bring people along.

There was a lot of negotiation. I had three or four pregnant women at the time, and I made them hire the pregnant women. I was like, "I'm not going to fuck up these working moms who are probably the breadwinners of their family."

I also negotiated a million dollars for me to pay people who weren't invited to go. I thought, "You're either going to get an offer for a job at Facebook, or I'm going to give you money." It was based on longevity; if the designer was with Hot for more than five years, I paid for a year's salary. Because I knew it was going to be really hard for people who loved the company and would see this as a betrayal.

And there *were* people who felt betrayed, because they believed in the company. And then I sold it. Some people hated Facebook even back then, so they saw it as being evil, an evil thing that I somehow stepped over my values.

There was a lot of negotiation. They low-balled me at first. I walked away from the deal. But I had a great team around me. I had my accountants. I had my M&A advisor, I had my lawyers. I had my team of people who've been fucked over by acquisitions before. I had a good bubble where I felt confident that I could negotiate because I had all of the context.

How about the money?

My bar was that, if I sell my company and it's the worst decision in the world, will I still walk away with a significant amount of money that's going to fundamentally change my life? If it didn't change my life, fundamentally, it wasn't going to be enough of a good deal for me.

And how did you do?

I remember when the check was mailed to me. It was a few million dollars. It was the biggest thing I've ever seen in my entire life. I took a picture of it. I still have that picture.

And I remember running upstairs, sitting in my bedroom; I have two young kids, they didn't know what was going on. [My partner] Scott and I go upstairs, I open this up and I see this fucking check for a few million dollars.

I was like: "I have a check.

That I'm going to bring to the bank.

And their eyeballs are going to fucking pop out of their heads."

And I remember going to the bank, dressed like this; I had been financially struggling for how many years? And I had this check...

How did that feel?

It was amazing. I'm so proud of how I conducted myself. I thought, this is a girl who a lot of people underestimated. Who went to art school. Who got a Bachelor's of Fine Arts degree. And competed in a man's world; I was one of just a few women leaders at that time.

And I negotiated the best fucking deal, without going to school for it.

And again, I have to thank the people who've been there before me and their generosity. Kevin Farnham shared his deals with me, Christopher Ireland was there for every step of the way. And I had other people who were checking in and they were like, "Make sure you do this and don't do that."

And then ultimately, I was the one who closed the deal. And so I'm incredibly proud of it. It put a marker in time. It was in the newspapers. Hot Studio made the news. John Maeda put me in the Design in Tech Report and said, "This is a change. This is a landscape change for designers." And I'm just super proud of it. And even though I did get to Facebook, and it wasn't the right fit for me, it worked out for a lot of other people.

So you got the cash up front; were there other terms of the deal related to compensation?

There was a certain number of people who had to stay in the company for three years. They listed my top employees by name. And so a percentage of them, if a percentage of them decided to leave, I would get less of an earnout. So, I had to make sure that those people were satisfied and happy.

And there was also a certain period of time I had to stay; four years.

But you didn't stay that long.

Facebook wasn't the right fit for me. I mean, we did the deal, but then it was a shit show. Integration was a shit show.

First of all, there were things that I didn't know about the deal. I was super optimistic. But what I didn't pay attention to were the people who were already in design at Facebook. I only met a few of them. My understanding was that they were really happy that Hot Studio was going to join them. But in reality it was a small group of designers, and they didn't think we were good enough.

They had a bias against agencies. There's a whole thing against agency versus product companies; that was alive and well at Facebook—they somehow didn't see the skills that we had as designers and agencies applying to product design. They thought it was a different animal. I mean, it's different, but it's just a different way of looking at problems. And so when we got to Facebook, there was not a welcome mat there.

And I was 50 years old. I was one of the oldest people at Facebook. I was older than Sheryl. Mark was 25 years old. His leadership team was 25 years old. They did not give a shit about the experience that I would bring to the table. It was more like, you're here. Now prove to me that you belong here. There was no real ramp up for me. There was no real support for me.

At the end of the day, it wasn't about me. They didn't really want me. They really wanted my worker-bee people. I was a strategic thinker who could think broadly. They needed people who were going to go narrow and deep and care about the pixels. So it was hard for them to place me to begin with. But they also didn't give me any kind of buffer or support or ramp me up. So a lot of my leaders, my leadership team struggled too. The people who were executing did well.

The people who were strategic really struggled finding a place. And some of them were pushed out early. That shook me because I felt like I was betraying them. I was afraid of getting fired. I didn't have support. No matter what I did, they didn't think I was performing well. The culture was too male, young male.

And then Autodesk came and offered me a job, and I used what my earnout was to negotiate a really good deal to move over to Autodesk.

So you did end up walking away from cash at Facebook?

I walked away from millions.

Wow. In retrospect, was that a good decision?

Does it hurt? Yes, when I think about it. But what did I trade? My sanity. I would have a lot more money today. My critical voice would be like, "Well, you're an idiot." But my sanity, my intuition is: "You saved yourself."

I regret none of it. I don't regret the acquisition because I am now financially secure. No, I don't have a yacht. I don't have property in France. I don't have any of it, but I have two kids in college that I'm paying for, full ride. I have a good life here. I don't really think about money. I work; I still work as a coach, but I have this financial security which I would never have had if I didn't sell my company to Facebook.

What would you have done differently?

There's always lessons learned. And so I think if I had to go back in time, I would have been less optimistic. I should have asked about culture fit. I should have asked to meet more of their designers. I should have asked about integration strategy. I didn't know any of that stuff. And I put too much faith into Facebook. I'm a person who always looks at the good news, but a little pessimism would've gone a long way.

Was there an integration plan prior to the deal closing?

There was no integration plan. We didn't have anything on paper. It was like people were rolling in, but Facebook... It was the early days of Facebook. They weren't organized. So they were rolling my team in and they were putting people on projects. And then it's up to the people who run those projects to make sure that my designers felt welcome there. And some people were just left hanging in the cold.

If I did this again, I would've asked for an integration plan. I would've asked more questions about the culture. And I would've asked who I was reporting to.

What advice would you give a designer who is thinking of selling their company?

Have a really good team of people around you who you trust, who have had the experience before, who get your company, and who get the things that are important to you. Not just financials, but culture and people, and your value system. It's super critical to have a great team around you.

And you have to find those people. You've got to find your mentors. That's how you grow. Find the people who've been in the experiences before, because it'll give you comfort and they'll help you prepare for the worst case. If you don't know them, look at your competitive space. Look at the people who you've competed with. And if they've gone through this, reach out. The worst thing that could happen is they say no. But you know what? People who go through acquisitions are more than willing to share their war stories.

You're suddenly in the church; it's very similar to having a child. When you don't have kids, and then you get pregnant and the baby's born, you step over a metaphorical line. You step into a community of people who understand the world you're in. That's what it's like with acquisition. When you are a founder or a CEO, we all know what keeps us up at night. We all have the same fears.

A lot of the downturn, when things were really bad, I would often go to bars with my competitors and we would commiserate. We compete for the same projects. And even in a downturn, that one project can keep your company. But we were all rooting for each other. We were supporting each other because we know how hard it is to run a company. There are fears. There's payroll. There's so much stuff that normal people don't have exposure to.

If you don't have that network, find the network.

Advisor Teams & Specialized Roles

Maria described an advisory team, or network, that helped her through the sale process. She included other founders who had successfully sold their companies, and made a point to recognize that those founders sold *design consultancies*, not just product companies. In addition, her advisory team included her accountant, her M&A advisor, and her lawyers.

This is the makeup of a strong advisory team. Let's look at each role, and what to look for when you assemble your team.

Include an M&A advisor or banker, to help you bring your company to market, find potential buyers, and structure your deal.

I never knew what it meant to be in "Mergers & Acquisitions" before considering selling my company; it always reminded me of George Costanza, from *Seinfeld*, getting into the very vague "Importing and Exporting." I learned that a) "M&A advisors" and "bankers" are terms used synonymously during this process, and b) without a banker, I would probably have been taken for a ride.

These are the things your M&A advisor or banker will do to help you in the process:

Develop your go-to-market story

Your company is a story, and designers are really good at telling *design* stories—stories of how people use and benefit from products and services. But we're often bad at telling stories that focus either on the purely financial, or on a broader business story. That's a banker's sweetspot: helping you explain to companies that you don't just make beautiful or meaningful design work—you act as a value multiplier, or contribute a set of ancillary skill sets, or expand market potential, or bring accretive revenue, or open the door to new client service pathways. They'll work with you to understand what you want out of a deal, and then help you tell the world your story in just the right way.

Connect you with potential buyers

A unique part of the sale process is the dating phase with potential buyers: the cat and mouse game of giving enough information to prospective buyers that they want to learn more, but not so much that they turn you down before they ever get to hear and learn the details. First, your banker will create a list of contacts that you may want to engage with. This is usually based on their "ear to the ground" knowledge; as they network, they learn about companies that are interested in growing design capabilities. They also have a set of contacts at the "usual suspects"—private equity firms, operational consultancies, and tech integrators. And, they'll ask if you have any specific companies you want to add to the list.

Next, they'll create a teaser—a one-pager that, without mentioning your company by name, gives a high level overview of the value you can provide. It highlights your company size, revenue, key capabilities, and any unique qualities about your firm. They'll email that to the whole list, and people who are interested in learning more will request the next document, a Confidential Information Memorandum (or CIM). The CIM is a 30–40 page document that adds color to the teaser by better describing who you are, what you do, and providing a deeper dive into your financials, customers, team, and unique parts of your company. Prepare yourself that it's going to look terrible; it's going to look as if a banker made it, not a designer.

When potential buyers show interest in the teaser, they'll then sign an NDA before receiving the CIM. The teaser was anonymous; the CIM is not. This is where the process starts to feel real, because there's now an indicator of your sale out in the world and out of your control. More about secrecy in later chapters; for now, suffice to say that many people ignore NDAs, and as I networked through my own process, I received numerous CIMs that I shouldn't have from people generous with their intentions, showing me how other companies presented themselves.

After seeing the CIM, some prospects will drop out, and the group that's left becomes the target of your roadshow—presentations that you give about yourself, highlighting your work and experience in the best light possible. This part probably isn't very hard, because as consultants, we present work all day long. But there's a lot riding on it, because often that first presentation can be what really sets a deal in motion. We'll go into more detail on the roadshow presentations themselves later in this book.

Your banker will backchannel information to you (from *their* banker, most likely) and as the process and conversations continue, they'll act as your advisor on how to shape and refine your message, which buyers are most serious or committed, and where they think you'll have the best outcome based on your goals and needs.

Structure your finances

While they're helping you show off your company, your banker will also be translating your finances into the format and style that a buyer will expect. I understand the financial fundamentals of running a business, but I had never produced documents for anyone to look at other than my partners and my accountant. Our banker's format followed what a buyer expected to see. He leveraged all of our Quickbooks data, and my various spreadsheets, to develop a working model which looks three years backwards.

He also spoke extensively with us about what would constitute a realistic forward-looking forecast, and the model included 18 months into the future. This was based on historic trends, pipeline, leads, and marketing events.

Structure the deal

Once a buyer has formally indicated their interest through a letter of intent, or LOI, your M&A advisor will do their magic: they'll negotiate on your behalf. They understand what's realistic and what the market will bear, they likely have a strong relationship with the seller's financial team, and they've (hopefully) done this enough times that they have a muscle memory for how a deal will work and what might make it fall apart. They'll be your advocate on when to push back and when to accept detailed financial issues, and they'll be a sounding board to role-play different scenarios related to those negotiations. Since they act as an intermediary between you and the buyer, you'll be able to vent to them and have them translate your anxiety or annoyances into productive steps forward. And they'll work with your attorneys on the nonfinancial part of the deal, when asked.

I found that having a banker on our team was critical to our success; just be prepared to pay them, perhaps more than you imagined. Terms are different depending on who you work with and how much your company is worth, and they only get paid if you actually sell, but expect to pay a minimum amount of hundreds of thousands of dollars, and more likely, a low percentage of the total deal size (anywhere from 3–7% seems to be typical).

I found my banker/advisor during my initial research. I looked at the various deals they had done in the past, and saw they had helped some companies that I recognized and respected. I'm extremely glad I selected someone who had experience with design companies, and experience with service businesses.

Include a certified public accountant, to help make sure you pay as little tax as possible.

Prior to our acquisition, our CPA helped us with the basics: filing our tax return at the end of the year. She understood our business, and our business was very simple, so we interacted rarely.

During the acquisition, and especially during the financial negotiations, we found ourselves communicating much more frequently. The biggest concerns we had, which she helped us through, were related to the tax implications of when and how to receive money. These are some of the specific things your CPA will help you with.

Double-check your books

As you get into diligence, which we'll talk through later in this book, an acquirer will be looking into your financial history with much more scrutiny than you are likely used to. We follow best practices with Quickbooks: connect to our credit cards and bank accounts, categorize things into accounts, and reconcile at the end of each month. But the books get a little more complicated at the end of each year, because closing balances are intertwined with revenue recognition methods. As your banker structures your financial outlook, you'll have to get very crisp on your revenue recognition method.

Advise you on the best way to receive payment

Your deal may contain a mixture of cash and stock, and there are implications on when you receive this compensation and how you report it to the IRS.

For example, stock has value, but you may not have earned that value when the deal closes (if it's tied to an earnout period). There's an IRS rule called an 83(b) which allows you to pay tax on the stock when it's granted, which—theoretically—will be at a lower value than when there's a liquidity event.

Or, your stock may be referenced as being made pursuant to Section 721, which describes that "No gain or loss shall be recognized to a partnership or to any of its partners in the case of a contribution of property to the partnership in exchange for an interest in the partnership." Yikes; I'm never going to be able to get my head around that.

Your CPA will help you work through the implications of filing an 83(b), will try to explain Section 721 to you, will take on all of the other arcane parts of the tax code, and remind you to actually follow through on the paperwork.

Include a lawyer, to negotiate your best deal possible.

While you can probably get by without an M&A advisor, and you may be able to work the tax implications yourself, there's no way you'll get through this process without a lawyer. The paperwork is just too thick and daunting, the language obscure, and the intimidation factor is off the charts. When you find a lawyer, look for someone who has done this before—worked through deals that focus on creative services, rather than products. And make sure they're small enough that you'll get their time and attention!

Here are some of the things your lawyer will do to help you in the process:

Translate the negotiated terms of the deal into a formal contract, and create the actual legal documents

Your banker is going to help you negotiate the financial parts of your deal. Your lawyer will help you negotiate everything else. For example, in an asset sale, you'll be selling everything the company owns, like the contracts you have in place with your clients. They'll help you write language to make sure that, while you'll do your best to provide all contracts, and to confirm that all contracts are buttoned up, you'll have an out if you made a mistake along the way. When my lawyer works on contracts, I frequently see him adding language like "to the best of my knowledge" or "within reason" and changing words like "all" or "every" to "all that I am aware of." I also see him arguing for like-terms: if the buyer gets something, the seller should get it, too.

Advise you on acceptable contract language and market comps

Just like your banker understands what other companies are being valued at, your lawyer understands what terms are common in contracts. I tried to educate myself on the things they were recommending, but there's a reason I'm not a lawyer; I struggled with terms like *wrong pocket assets* and a much more robust *indemnification section* than I've typically seen. For example, imagine that your contract has a clause that looks like this:

> *Procedures for Indemnification of Third Party Claims. A Purchaser Indemnified Party entitled to indemnification hereunder with respect to a third-party claim may assume the defense and otherwise deal with such claim in good faith, with counsel of its choice; provided that, such Purchaser Indemnified Party shall not settle any such third-party claim without the prior written consent of the Indemnifying Party (which consent shall not be unreasonably withheld, delayed or conditioned), unless such claim involves Losses which are reasonably expected to be in excess of an amount indemnifiable hereunder due to the application of the Cap.*

You may find yourself watching a back-and-forth negotiation over the last sentence, *"unless such claim involves Losses which are reasonably expected to be in excess of an amount indemnifiable hereunder due to the application of the Cap."* It's very satisfying to not have to engage in those discussions and trust that someone else knows what they're doing!

Scenario-play different worst-case outcomes of various post-close events

Designers are typically skilled at scenario-play because a big part of our job is thinking about or drawing things that don't yet exist and then considering the implications of those innovations or changes. Your lawyer will lead you through similar exercises, mostly related to worst-case scenarios. These scenarios then lead to proposed contract changes, feeding that negotiation process.

For example, consider what happens if, post-close, a client from several years back sues you for designing something that isn't accessible for people with visual impairments. Imagine that the MSA covering that client interaction is still active, and as part of the acquisition, you've assigned the contract to your buyer. Who is responsible for covering the legal costs for the lawsuit, and who will be held liable if you are deemed to be in the wrong? There are countless things like this that, while unlikely, *could* happen. In the excitement of a deal, it's easy to want to see a future that works perfectly. Your lawyer will work you through a future that is more uncertain.

Be "bad cop"

After a deal has closed, you get to (or have to) work with the people who acquired you in close proximity and collaboration. If they have a bad taste in their mouth from the negotiation process of the deal, it's going to make those interactions difficult. The negotiation is, in some respects, a prolonged job interview, where your behavior will color the way you are perceived. It's great to have someone else push back on things, because (right or wrong), they'll be perceived as the person who is difficult to work with, not you.

There's a limit to this pushback, and at some point in the negotiation, you'll arrive at details where your lawyer will advise you that it's not worth it. Later, we'll talk about the importance of establishing non-negotiables before starting the legal process. These are the places where your bad-cop lawyer will carry the burden of pushback, so you can keep your reputation intact.

Include design leaders who, to quote Maria, had been "fucked over by acquisitions before."

Acquisitions are unique, and aren't something we encounter frequently in our lives. But we can lean on our friends and professional acquaintances and learn from their experiences, in order to fill in the gaps of our knowledge and level the negotiating playing field. And as Maria said, those who have had negative experiences are probably going to be straight with you.

Your team of "been there, done that" advisors will help you with a few key parts of the process.

Share the terms of their deal

As I researched this book, I found that some people are more forthcoming than others, but none of the people I interviewed were willing to share the actual contracts they signed that described the deal, or even get close to that level of specificity. But some of my personal friends were, and it was invaluable to me. It's not The Big Number that's the most useful, although it's helpful to have a financial context. Instead, it's the nitty gritty of all of the small ways that might chip away at the upside of your deal.

These "been there, done that" people will also be able to give you context with which to compare *your* deal, and talk through the comparison with you. I think this is one of the most helpful parts of discussing your experience with someone else. I mentioned earlier that I felt like I was "doing it wrong" all the way through the process. Having a point of reference made me see that I was, at least at a high level, working from the same set of assumptions and considerations as someone who "did it right."

Help you work through each decision along the way

While there's certainly a set of common steps to a process (and I hope this book will help you learn about those commonalities), each step is also extremely unique and tied to the context of your company, and each step needs to be handled with care and introspection. Your team of once-bitten-twice-shy advisors can help you make those decisions thoughtfully, and can help you spend your limited time and energy in the right places. Maria described that her advisors helped direct her energy, giving her advice to "Pay attention to this, don't pay attention to that."

It's also likely that you solve problems in a similar way as those advisors, and that you speak the same language when it comes to evaluating a situation. Your conversations with them will feel more lucid than those with your bankers and lawyers, and I found these interactions to be much more relatable.

For example, when I started talking about financial projections, other design leaders could relate to the more intuitive or flexible nature of a sales pipeline, which—as you'll hear later from Doreen Lorenzo, the former CEO of frog design, is "a very fluid pricing model. And it's really dependent on how much business you have at that moment or how much you can charge a client. It's about the value you are going to bring to the company through the project. And that model is just insane to some people." A banker, and buyer, will want a very objective view of future sales. Other design leaders are comfortable discussing the more realistic nature of design sales.

Give you moral support

A big part of working through a complex problem is commiserating, and sometimes, you don't want someone to solve a problem—you want them to empathize with you, and simply "be on your team." If you have partners at your company, they play this role, but outside and trusted advisors can really help work through some of the long parts of the process. There are parts of the process that feel truly defeating. Am I doing the right thing for myself and my team? Is the buyer going to walk away? Why aren't they responding to my texts? Your creative advisory team can be that shoulder on which to bitch and moan.

Potentially talk you out of it

I spoke with several design leaders who didn't sell their companies, but got fairly far through the process. They described that, while a decision to back away is complicated, they were able to come to that decision after meaningful reflection with a trusted peer. Strong leaders know that being surrounded by "yes-men" isn't healthy, and that multiple perspectives from educated people lead to more valuable decision making. You'll be flying high on adrenaline and optimistic about an exciting new chapter in your career. Negative sentiments, while disappointing to hear, can help you evaluate your decision with a more objective, rational, and clear perspective.

Your role

You'll play a few roles in the group. First and foremost, it's your company, and so your most important role is having an opinion and speaking up for yourself. When you don't understand something, it's on *you* to stop the train and get someone to explain it. When you're feeling pushed around or intimidated, it's on *you* to be loud, forceful and direct. And if the process isn't going the way you want, it's *your* responsibility to fix it. It's easy to find yourself going along for the ride, because there are so many moving parts that feel intimidating or confusing. If the process has gained too much inertia in one direction, it can become harder and harder to undo. It's ultimately your process, just like it's your company.

Additionally, you'll play the role of *advocating for urgency*. No matter how much the people on your advisory team care about you and the outcome of the sale, the sale isn't their first priority. Your lawyer and CPA have other clients. Your banker is pushing on multiple deals at once. And your acquirer is looking to minimize the risk of their investment, and so they'll likely be methodical and slow. Ultimately, there's no real hurry to get a deal done, except that I've found that the longer a deal of any kind hangs around unsigned, the less likely it is to ever get signed at all. The world changes, the people involved in the negotiation come and go, and so once you've made a decision (small or big), it's in your best interests to push forward.

That advocating for urgency is shown primarily through communications. Be in touch with each party with regularity. Send follow-up emails to check on status. Get people's phone numbers, and text with some regularity. Schedule regular meetings and check-ins, and come to those meetings with an agenda. This will all likely come naturally, because you're already in the services business and these are all things we do when interacting with clients. But it can be easy to abdicate this communication responsibility to one of the other parties (often the banker), which will slow the process.

You'll be in charge of *being the connector.* Your CPA, lawyer, and banker often need to speak to each other, but this becomes a selective dance since at least two of the three are likely charging you by the hour. Not everyone needs to know everything. As a guideline, if it pertains to money, everyone needs to chime in; if it's about value (what you give and what you get), it's likely a lawyer/banker item; and if it's about what-if scenarios ("What if I get fired after the acquisition?" or "What if I change my mind?"), it's solidly one for the lawyer.

You'll also likely find yourself *playing a game of telephone*, with you in the middle. Your lawyer may have a question that is best answered not by the buyer's lawyer but by the buyer's executive champion or stakeholder. They probably won't reach out directly, so you'll have to do it. I found myself frequently fielding questions from my attorney, jumping on the phone with my banker, and then texting the results back. It's not an ideal role to be in, but— again, since it's your process—you'll want to know what's going on, and the best way to know is by being smack in the middle of it all.

Finally, since you'll wear the anxiety, it will be your responsibility to reach out to your mentors, friends and fellow designers when you need a hug. They probably aren't going to proactively come to you, but I'll bet they will be forthcoming with support!

Gavin Lew, Who Founded User Centric and Sold It to GfK in 2012

Our next conversation is with Gavin, who started User Centric, a user experience consultancy, in 1999. In 13 years, he grew the company to over 60 people. He sold the company in 2012 to GfK, a German consumer research company with over 10,000 employees in over 200 offices around the world. He remained at GfK for close to 6 years before leaving to found Bold Insight.

Gavin, what was the context of your acquisition?

In 1999, I started a company called User Centric. We focused on UX research and design, before UX was a known acronym and name. User Centric offered research methodologies that were different from market research. We were behavioral scientists. About four years into it, I met Tara Bosenick, founder of the German company SirValUse. Tara said, "I think global UX will be big and you guys are just like my team in Germany, kind of a small, niche company."

Tara's company was bought by GfK which was the fourth largest market research firm in the world. As part of that deal, she said, "I need to buy User Centric." So GfK was the acquisition vehicle for a little German company to merge with a little US company and form a global product group.

Why were you exploring an acquisition?

Being a small consultancy can be tough. There were a couple moments, like in 2001 or 2008 when the world essentially shut down, where our survival was in question. Coming out of other dry spells between 2008 to 2012, there were periods of fallow years. Owning a business comes at great personal risk because at the end of the day, owners are personally responsible for real estate leases. Leases are a pretty big part of operating costs. Beyond leases, there are salaries; salaries are a consultancy's greatest cost. As all businesses, cash flow can be challenging, even for profitable businesses, because it is based on timing. If we don't get timely payments, we could not make payroll. If we don't make payroll, something bad happens. The team morale, the culture... it changes your world.

In times of crisis, you are reminded of risk. During the financial crisis of 2008, we had to reduce staff. When we had an opportunity to form a global UX practice within a large company, we said, "Okay, why don't we just take all the risk off the table, get a good salary and maybe blow the doors off and make an incredible global team? Take the acquirer's MSAs, their sales staff, and let's build something amazing."

Tell me a little about the financial structure of the deal.

The valuation is pretty classic. It's a multiple to top line and a multiple to EBITDA. Our multiple was above one. In other countries, they can go for multiples well above one and sometimes closer to two. It just depends on the markets and in some ways the mood of the market.

Did you have an earnout?

I did. The earnout was partial upfront, and then partial on the backend of three years. It was based on a few things: the global revenue, the internal revenue that you actually generated, and profit. Elements were weighted. This was a win because risk was mitigated, the team was intact, and growth expectations were reasonable.

If I could offer advice, it would be that the elements that you previously took for granted must be controlled, if your earnout has an EBITDA component. You need to hold as many factors that contribute to EBITDA constant on your earnout, and understand the variables that go into EBITDA. As business owners, we just do really good work and we leave the accounting to others and that's the area where the buyer can take advantage. I knew the costs of things that I paid for when I owned my company. But being part of a larger organization, control over costs can be pooled and weighted in ways that I did not consider. For example, as a business owner, pre-sale, you know how much your monthly lease payment is. You know your total IT expenditures across a year. You know your legal costs. But as part of a large organization, these costs could be aggregated across the organization and allocated by headcount. So your monthly lease costs are part of an aggregate and you are not responsible for just your monthly, but the aggregate across the organization divided by headcount.

Imagine you're a lean and efficient organization prior to acquisition—now your IT, legal, real estate, HR costs go from actual to a per-head cost that may be different and these differences impact your EBITDA.

But if it's an acqui-hire, it's the value of your people. Can you retain the critical people? Do you want to cash some money out and give it to them on the side? If you do side deals with your top people, will that come out of your pot? Or will the company plan for retention bonuses during the first or second year of acquisition?

You want to negotiate that upfront and say, "Look, here's what I'm going to do. In order to hit my numbers, to make you happy and make me happy, I need these people and I need this kind of money to keep them." How much of it can you get from the sale price versus what you're going to pull out of your own sale price?

Another bit of advice is to have your earnout based on what you can control. My example—and I should have seen it—I didn't make all my earnout. It didn't hit 100% and that was because one of our weighted variables was global revenue, which I didn't have full control over. My counterparts in other countries flatlined and I'm like, "Had you just gone up a little bit, I would've hit my earnout." Control what you can control. That's easy to say in hindsight.

It seems like a lot rides on committing to key metrics, before really knowing the dynamics of how you'll achieve those metrics.

Most businesses are cash-based. We went from cash-based to accrual, and a different form of accrual, which is German, called the International Financial Reporting Standards, or IFRS. I was naïve to IFRS. I did not understand the difference. A lot of businesses count cash when it gets in the door. IFRS will count cash on an accrual basis.

Design agencies tend to bill by the month, versus 50 upfront and 50 at the end. We would bill 50/50, and that could be a significant number that's not counted. We would get money and hit a certain number, but with the IFRS standards, it takes a while to accrue. We're like, "Whoa, that's revenue." And they're like, "No, it's not revenue until it accrues in the standard accounting principles." We would respond, "That's not how we counted." But even if we got paid upfront, we only get credit for what we accrued. It's great for cash flow, but it's not been accrued.

What are some of the things you encountered after the acquisition that you weren't expecting, and that weren't so great?

IT, real estate, finance, salaries... you'll never get another chance to rightsize all those things. I should have considered that HR would now involve a corporate process, and I no longer controlled it. You are told that you have control over your business, but when you add corporate processes, you will find that things that are easy become challenging. Before closing the deal, I should have executed more changes.

Hypothetically, what if the HR data says your people are overpaid, but you aren't privy to or in control of this data? As an organization, you hire employees who come in with expectations and see departures due to salary. If you feel that your team is leaving because they can get higher salaries elsewhere, then there is a disconnect.

As a business owner, when you are not able to adequately compensate those who are knowledgeable, trained and loyal, the business loses the talent. The outcome is that good people quit for money somewhere else and then you have to hire someone off the street who needs to be trained. This is the flawed logic that hurts the time and effort spent developing organic talent. If you lose that power, then you will spend a lot of resources as attrition occurs.

Here is another hypothetical—one to be considered during acquisition negotiation. Consider your Information Technology costs. You know the annual cost, because you pay it. But when you are acquired, actual costs do not apply. Finance might give a per-head allocation, similar to real estate. I will be the first to say that this "per-head allocation" might be higher than you could imagine as a small business owner.

Say you had 100 employees. If your IT allocation was $10,000 per employee then that is $1 million. As a business owner, IT tends to be laptops and communication devices/services. If laptops are cycled every 3–4 years, you know the costs. But across a major corporation, there are other costs and when they are aggregated with IT salaries, the "allocation" that is placed on your P&L can be much, much higher than what you expect. The impact of this is that your EBITDA is saddled with much higher costs, which lowers your profit. But nothing in your business substantially changed. Your profit went down, and if your earnout is based on a profit target, then you made a miscalculation.

If your earnout is based on profit, there are lots of variables that go into it. IT, and real estate, and other financial things where you can get into the aggregate, of which I had no idea of the impact that these charges would have to profit. You need to lock those things down in your P&Ls. If you're being purchased based on your profits and you're giving projections based on those models, you have to hold as many things constant as you can (or at least variable within reason), or you're going to not make profit because you're getting pulled into the aggregate.

What are some of the things you had to give up after the acquisition?

When you run a business, you have discretionary income—whether it be a car, or the use of a red carpet club in a lounge in an airport. There are lots of things that, from an expense side, you can take personally and benefit from. That's discretionary income. All of that goes away.

Things that you had absolute control over could now be in the hands of other organizations. Let's say you had an initiative where you worked with a university to recruit strong candidates; it was successful and you wanted to do it again, so you presented a plan to leadership. And they applauded it because, comparing how much it costs to acquire a handful of people, and I can do it for hundreds of dollars? Everyone said, "no-brainer." And what if it took not a month, but over a year to get that initiative funded because action sat in another organization? There are politics, power and influence levers that you didn't have to navigate when you ran your business.

You've described some issues that seem to have had a pretty significant impact on your ability to manage your team. In hindsight, were there places in the sale process that you feel you could have headed these off?

I took people at their word for things. I asked them, "What if there is a major change in corporate structure? My earnout should pay out at 100%." They said, "We've had hundreds of acquisitions. It's never happened."

Be strong. Or have your legal counsel be stronger. Consider responding, "I hear exactly what you're saying, and if that's true, then there should be no problem for you to put it in writing. If there is no risk of it happening, then you should be fine signing it." During negotiations, it is all about position, not acquiescence. Negotiation is the one time to lock in what you want to control.

There's a whole page and a half of definitions in the contract. Know how they define revenue and profit, and how those can be manipulated. These definitions are key. Your assumptions need to be written down. I could easily see the scenarios where it could have been devastating.

There's just a lot of strategies that I did not consider prior to the final contract. In some ways, lawyers could have helped, but they have to know the behind the scenes financials of your particular business to identify where to place hard caps or ratios that should be applied. When you are in negotiation, you go in thinking that everyone's going to be great. You want educated counsel to be that "cutthroat lawyer" who tells you where you have risk to have a lower EBITDA or clauses which could have disastrous impact if control is lost. These are business elements that you know, but may not have articulated aloud. The contract is where everything needs to be clear.

I thought, "I taught at a university, so is that considered another job? Am I still allowed to do that, or am I violating my employment agreement? What are the terms?" And your employment agreement doesn't always sync very well with your purchase agreement, so you've got to align those.

When you reflect on your experiences, what sort of advice would you give an owner who is contemplating a sale?

Consider what the end game is for your personal finances. Selling can take risk off the table. But the first step that anyone should think of is, after taxes and after shareholder partitions, is it worth it? If you sell your company for a million, after taxes, it's going to be $500,000. Is $500,000 worth it? Where is that threshold?

Is this a situation where you still need to work, or where you are going to retire? If the number is less than your target, then why not just keep going? That's the one thing I think people have to really think about. At what point does it become worth it? Because if you think about the acquisition, they're going to pay you some money upfront. That's their biggest risk. But in an earnout, depending upon the terms, depending upon how you hit your targets, you'll get more money, but it will come from the profit of your business unit.

During the five or six years that I was at GfK, I knew that my team made more money in profit to the acquiring company, than I did with my earnout. This is an example of what could happen if you are successful. Ask yourself: is the earnout large enough to make it worth the effort and change? Are you okay that the acquiring company will be paying you through your own profit?

For me, the advantages—reducing risk, and global growth—outweighed the concerns and it was a win-win.

Valuations & Multiples

Often, the first and biggest question on the minds of someone contemplating a sale is "How much money am I going to make?" There's no exact formula for this, but there are general guidelines and heuristics you can follow to come to a conclusion about the value of your company. And while there are many factors that go into a valuation of your company, the biggest are typically your financial history, your financial projections, and the multiple related to your revenue or earnings.

Preliminary financial model

To arrive at a valuation, you'll need a comprehensive financial model. This is something your banker will create in close collaboration with you (and your CFO, if you have one), and here are some of the things it will include:

Three or four years of historic, real revenue and earnings data

A buyer is going to want to see steady (and hopefully, better-than-linear) growth, so they'll want to see three years of historic data. They'll look for this in aggregate, month by month, and organized by client. The more you organize yourself now, the less time you'll spend waiting for either your banker or CPA to make sense of your mess. As our company grew I learned how to keep better financial books, but my early organization was... not great. I didn't adopt Quickbooks in earnest in the first few years of our business, and so as our financial modeling started, I had to move information from various spreadsheets into a central place. It's time consuming, but I found it cathartic as well: it was a good "walk down memory lane" for me to see just how much the company had grown and changed.

A projection of growth for the next two or three years

Your company valuation is going to be based on not just where you've been, but where you are going, and the likelihood that you'll get there. Your financial model will include a forward-looking view of growth, likely for the next two years.

There's a dance that plays out here between "realistic" and "optimistic." You want to present a very positive view of ability for growth, because it's attractive to a buyer and because it will increase the valuation of your company. But you'll be held to the numbers you are presenting, and it's very likely that a portion of the money you will earn from the sale will be tied to your achieving those projections.

A buyer will be looking not just for growth, but also relative predictability. Where possible, you'll see your financial model morph and shift to become less lumpy and more consistent. This, again, is a dance: will you actually be able to deliver on a model that has that type of uniformity?

Cost of sale (including real salaries and supporting salaries for projected growth), and expenses

Your historic model and your forecast will also include your expenses, with a particular lens on salaries. In a service business, the majority of our expenses are in our people (and the building they sit in), and if you project growth in the future, you'll need to propose realistic growth in your headcount expenses, too.

Part of these costs will also come from unexpected places. Gavin described overhead—"internal taxes"—that he wasn't expecting pre-sale, but that suddenly had a material impact on his numbers. These are points to probe on during negotiation, and to get in writing. What fees or expenses are shared across an organization? How much are they? And when, and how much, will they change in the future?

I've also found that salary expectations can vary tremendously in different industries. We'll hear later from Crystal Rutland who explains how, when she sold Particle Design to Wind River, she had to make a concerted effort *at the board level* to pay her employees what she forecasted.

Add backs

An "add back" is a strange element in a financial model that is used to improve the way your historic earnings look. These are one-time expenses that are, theoretically, anomalous; these are costs that are removed from your revenue (making your earnings look higher), because the acquiring company won't ever have to incur them again.

For example, if you held a large event like a conference and spent $100,000 on it, and that conference will never happen again—it was a one-time activity—you can deduct that from your expenses in the year in which it was held.

This is a lever that gives you a little more control over how your company is perceived, and a little more finesse over showing a consistent, non-lumpy burn rate. But these add backs have to be real, and too many of them set off alarm bells with buyers.

A set of assumptions that support your projection

If you've steadily improved your revenue by 15% year-over-year, it will seem highly unrealistic to suddenly project continual 40% growth post-acquisition, and a buyer will look for a narrative of your assumptions to explain that growth. Are you going to change your marketing strategy? How do you know it will work? Have you been turning away work, but now you feel you'll be able to handle that growth? Can you show examples? These assumptions may be listed in a separate document; more importantly, you'll need to be able to speak to them confidently and consistently in-person, and show real examples to support your expectations.

One big assumption you may make is that you'll be leveraging the buyer's sales team or pipeline to achieve new revenue targets. If that's the case, it's important to understand, in detail (and captured in writing) how that will work, what will be made available to you, and a realistic view of what upside that might bring. As you'll see in our next interview, Christian Barnard ran head first into competing sales approaches post-acquisition, and so any assumption of co-selling in support of higher revenue went out the window.

Notes to explain revenue recognition methods

Gavin described encountering a new accounting format that changed the way revenue was recognized, and that meant that he didn't hit his numbers:

revenue he expected to get in a current year would actually be recognized in the subsequent year. Having supportive notes on your current profitability approach will help bring these differences to light during negotiations, rather than after it's too late.

These are common recognition methods:

- Revenue is considered "earned" when money is received in the bank. This is not a great approach, because all of that money is at risk and is a liability, and your banker will have you change this (and that may be a pain, historically, because you'll have to revise all of the historic recognition in the model).

- Revenue is considered "earned" when the work is done. This form of accrual implies that you are tracking what "done" means. If your work is deliverable based, that's fairly easy: done means that the artifact (the comp, wireframes, powerpoint, product design) has been handed off to the client. If your work is billed hourly, done means when the hours have been burned.

- Revenue is considered "earned" when the work is done *and* the money is in the bank. This method of cash accounting is theoretically the easiest to prove, but gets messy for work in progress, or clients who are consistently delinquent in their payment.

But in all cases, you'll need to be prepared to substantiate your method during diligence: you'll need to show contracts with deliverables and dates assigned that match with invoices, or utilization reports that show hours worked per project. In many small companies, it's common that designers work on multiple projects at once. Real time tracking, through an automated tool, will make it much easier to show revenue was recognized as described.

Whatever the method, be prepared to talk about it with confidence, and to show examples that support how it's been applied consistently.

Valuation: The Big Number

Now that you have a pretty strong idea of your finances, and a good prediction of where they're going, you can arrive at a valuation: the Big Number. It's this number from which you negotiate; once the number is established, it's very difficult to change it in your favor (although, as you'll see in some of our stories, it's very easy for the potential purchaser to change it in *their* favor). The way the number is calculated can seem complicated, and while there are guidelines and heuristics for it, there's a lot that's very subjective and open to interpretation. But the biggest factors will be your revenue, your earnings, your contracts and your employees, with the largest weight on the finances. And the biggest lever will be on the "multiple."

Notes to explain client consolidation and anomalies

It's fairly common for a small services company to rely on one or two key anchor clients. For example, you'll later read that Max Burton, who sold his company to Fjord, worked very closely with Carnival Cruise Line and it was his major account. This speaks to the strong relationships you form during your work, which is great—but it presents a risk to a prospective buyer: what if that client goes away? If you can show a pathway to growth of alternative clients, or broad penetration in that anchor client's organization (working with multiple business units and stakeholders), it will help minimize fear of this consolidation.

An additional red flag for a buyer will be seeing an anomalous project value. If you consistently sign projects that are $100,000, and then have a single project that you signed for $500,000, you'll be asked to explain the unique nature of the program.

Multiples

The result of all of the financial modeling is to arrive at real revenue and EBITDA numbers, but these numbers don't translate directly to the value of your company; instead, they act as one of the key baselines upon which you can negotiate. To get to the financial value based strictly on your financials, your banker will identify a *multiplier* against your numbers. And ideally, your multiple is high and positive, although a negative multiple is sometimes applied for a company that's lacking leverage or that looks like it's in poor shape.

What to expect

A simple example shows the power of the multiple. If your revenue was one million dollars, a 1x multiple values your company at a million dollars. 2x indicates a value of two million, and so-on.

You've probably heard of massive valuations of internet startups. These valuations are often based on multiples of 5x for slow growth startups, 10x for a mid-growth company, and even 20x for startups growing like unicorns. But typically, service companies like design consultancies are valued anywhere from 1x to 3x revenue. The reason for the lower valuation is because of the constraints on scaling; theoretically, a product company can scale their revenue at a much higher (and even exponential) rate than their expenses, while a service business runs into a linear relationship between revenue and salaries.

1x and 3x revenue is still quite broad, and this is your room for negotiation. Often, the figure that's selected is based on comparable companies that have sold recently: their size, their revenue, their location, and the type of work they do. The rub here is that those figures aren't always publicly shared, and so you'll lean heavily on your banker to provide the initial number.

Sometimes, multiples are based on earnings instead of revenue, and these multiples may be 6x or 7x. Theoretically, a valuation based on revenue indicates that the company is able to sell work and less emphasis is placed on margins; this might be a strategic acquisition, where the operational efficiency is less important than a strong brand and reputation.

You will be held to this later!

The biggest takeaway of the financial modeling and multiple conversation is that this valuation number acts as a definitive flagpole that is really hard to move later. When you're working on these financial issues, it's very early in your sale and it's easy to gloss over just how binding and lasting this calculation is in the process. But once a financial model is presented to a prospective buyer, and once your banker has a good view of how you'll be valued, it's unlikely you can walk it back. Take your time to get this right, even if it means slowing down the momentum of the sale, and curbing your enthusiasm.

Christian Barnard, Who Was the COO at T3 When It Was Acquired by LRW/Material+ in 2019

Christian's done his tour of big design, with stops at Scient, frog, and Sapient (twice, first as Sapient in the early 2000s, and then more recently as Publicis Sapient). He also co-founded and sold two small design firms: Buzzbait in 1997, and Deft in 2012. After his role as Group Vice President at Razorfish, he took over operations at T3, and saw the company through its growth, and eventual sale in 2019.

Tell me a little about your experience at T3.

I joined T3 in 2015 as the Chief Operating Officer. T3 was a family owned, digitally focused design and innovation firm offering end-to-end services in brand design, product design, and loyalty and CRM. When I started, the company was doing about 20 million in revenue. In the years I was there, we grew to about 40 million in revenue. We had physical offices in Atlanta, New York, Austin, and we had about 250 people at the end of 2019.

The company was 25 years old, and had a very strong creative culture, a very founder-led culture. At that time, the two co-founders—Gay and Lee Gaddis—were taking a step back. Their son, Ben—who had been with the company for a few years and was the Chief Innovation Officer—came in to be the President. And the culture there was very familial. I hate saying that, and it bothered me when leadership would say, "Hey, we're a family," because we're not; it's ultimately a company and a team and a business. But some people were there for a very long time. The Chief Creative Officer was there for 25 years. In the creative industry we are in, that's very rare.

And the company did have a very "we'll take care of each other" vibe to the culture. We created these t-shirts that said *fiercely independent.* And that was part of our jam; it allowed us to do great creative work without robot overlords of holding companies and things like that.

Overall, T3 was the best job I've ever had! The people were great, the founders were very generous, the culture was fantastic, and the work we were doing was truly innovative. That experience will be hard to replicate. If any of the founders from T3 are reading this right now, I would like to thank you for the opportunity!

It sounds like everything was working great; but then, T3 sold to LRW Group in 2019. How did that deal happen?

I was out with Ben one day and he asked me, "What do you think if we were to take the company to the market and sell it?" Although this was a surprise to me, I can't imagine how long the family had thought about the decision, and how tough it was for them to move forward with any kind of sale.

So, we started meeting with bankers who facilitated the entire matchup.

Ben and I decided that because the culture was so strong and because of that fiercely independent piece of it, we were just going to do this with the two of us. Not many other people on the leadership team knew what we were doing. The family knew, but no one else on the executive team or company knew. We started going through the paces, meeting with bankers. We did our pitch deck, we did our CIM. And then we brought our CFO in, because as you know, it's all about the financials. Then it was the three of us. And then Ben and I started going out and meeting with potential buyers, big companies, holding companies, private equity companies. We did probably over a dozen of these meetings. And they asked for all the things: What's your pipeline look like? What's your recurring revenue? What's your profit? What are your growth plans? And things like that.

It was probably three to four months doing this somewhat covertly. And of the 16 that we met with, there were 12 companies of interest that were like, here's an offer on the table. As things moved along, and became more real, we brought more of the leadership team into the conversations, which helped out a lot.

One of the buyers—LRW Group—was positioning themselves to be a platform. Their leadership team had already made about 9 acquisitions before T3. Some really small, some bigger, and at the time, T3 was the largest targeted acquisition. Their intent was end-to-end digital services, research, creative agency, marketing, product design, brand design, loyalty and CRM.

It seemed like a good complement, and the LRW leadership team was very impressive; we liked them a lot. We met with them several times during diligence. And the T3 owners made the decision to go with them.

What happened right after the deal closed?

The deal completed on October 31st, 2019. We communicated it to the team, and we had to figure out how to go from "fiercely independent" to "fiercely part of a larger organization." And that's where one of the learnings comes in. It was a bit of shock, which I think led to a bit of lack of trust with the team. Those deals don't just happen; they take a long time. And now the majority of teams, especially the leadership team, knew that we were in those conversations for a long time and not many people knew about it.

So I think there was a bit of a trust deficit as an outcome of the way the communication was handled, and I would handle that differently next time. It was better received than I thought, and we didn't have a lot of turnover immediately after the transaction went through. And from my perspective, we were still operating T3 as an independent company within a larger holding company. The LRW leadership team and the PE firm were great to work with through the entire process.

When did you start to integrate the teams?

COVID accelerated a lot of integration. We went through an integration process, and T3 took the lead as the company to integrate with four of the smaller companies that focused on making things. We went through role alignment and operational alignment. We asked the different companies, "What are your operations? How do you go to market? What's your sales process?" And then, as a combined entity, we operated as about an $80 million division.

But there were serious challenges with this. Some of them were cultural, some of them were procedural and a lot of them were communications.

For example, things like title and level: Executive Creative Director (ECD) here and Executive Creative Director there are two very different things. ECD in this one company was just a few years out of school. ECD in this other company meant 25 years of experience. And we had to do compensation alignment to rationalize some of that stuff.

Culturally, the companies were very, very different. There was a company in Seattle, one in San Francisco, one in Philadelphia. And the culture was very different not just because of geography, but because they were all founder-led organizations and those founders instilled different cultures in each one of them.

As an example, things like vacation time became a real challenge. We told the different companies, "Keep your own vacation policies and holidays." But T3 had more vacation time. We would try to set up a meeting and some people said, "Well, we have that day off," and someone else would respond, "Well, we have the next two days off." And everyone asked, "How's that supposed to work? That's not cool."

Little things like that seem little, but are actually very, very important big things when it's a people-based business, and especially a creative business. So we had to create an integration plan and we had to create equitable treatment for everybody.

T3 had 250 people, the majority of whom were focused on their craft. Those people said, "As long as I get to continue doing cool work and great work and you're not going to impact my ability to do that good work, it's okay." But as those teams started coming together and working on projects together, that's when we started to see culture clash.

For instance, the acquiring company LRW was a research company. It was very, very performance-driven, a culture of "results, go, go, go, go, go results." And although we grew at a healthy clip at T3, it wasn't the same go-get-'em culture. It was more like, "Hey, we're going to do more great work."

One example was that we got rid of our time tracking. And I think LRW looked at us saying, "You guys are a bunch of children running around. You don't have a lot of operational rigor or client rigor in your business." I think they looked down on us; in response, we started to get the opinion of, "Well, these guys are stuffy, and they're not creative."

Here's another example. LRW had a sales system whereby they asked all their leadership team to send out a number of outbound emails to targets and prospects. In their leadership meetings, they would pull up the scoreboard and say, "Jen sent out 20 emails last week and got one meeting."

For what they were selling, it works really well. Just more widgets. You could send a blast email and say, "Need research done on some topic?" And sell that. They explained to us that, "We've had a proven sales system; you guys need to start doing it, too."

And we responded, "That's never going to work." If I go to our Chief Creative Officer and say, "Look, I need you to send out 20 emails to people via LinkedIn," he's going to say, "No way." And then the question is, "Well, Christian, why can't you make them do it?"

Well, because we don't do work that way. And that's not how we sell business. That's not how we win business, how we deliver business. That's not how we start a relationship with a client. Mandate culture to use a selling system that doesn't feel right? That was a massive cultural divide.

The delivery culture was another example of a big difference in how work gets done. A lot of their projects had a very, very tight project plan. You followed that project plan linearly. They looked at our work and said, "That's a mess." It's not a mess; it's iterative and it's creative and sometimes we don't even know what we're going to do before we do it.

Do you think these things are possible to resolve without some sort of autocratic, top-down force?

I want to say yes, but my heart and my gut say no. That's really hard to do unless the cultures are so closely aligned. We saw that with frog and Aricent, right? You try bringing engineers and creatives together, which makes sense to people in the boardroom at a private equity company. They think, "Oh, you design stuff, and they build stuff; just smash them together."

In the case of frog and Aricent, there were legit language, time zone, and cultural barriers. But even after you work through that—and I *do* think that part is workable—it's really about why people join a company, what they think is meaningful and important, and that's your culture. Join frog for a reason, join Aricent for a reason, join T3 for a reason. The reason that we spend our time doing work and making things is different. And those things are difficult to align.

The opportunity for success, and the reason why we brought those different companies together with T3, was that we're all doing creative work in some flavor and form, but we're just doing it differently. I was hopeful that integration of these companies would be easier. But it's still really hard because you're changing the foundation of why people are there in the first place.

The companies LRW had acquired, including T3, were small, founder-led organizations. It starts there. You might have better success if you make the acquisition, chop off the founder level, and say, "Okay, we're going to take these clients and these people and those clients and those people, and we're going to start something fresh, net new." As opposed to having these founder-led cultures coming together and trying to work, which is really, really, really difficult.

The other thing we did is a massive communication plan to our clients. We said to them, "Look: that company that you've been working with for 15 years is about to be acquired by another company. You're still getting the same people, the same level of service. Don't worry about that." But clients feel that too. They would worry, "Oh shit, you're going to change." And in fact, it did change the way that we work with them.

About 2 years into the integration, LRW leadership decided to rebrand the company, transitioning all of the legacy companies it had acquired to a new brand called Material. I was part of that rebranding effort, it was really fascinating and exciting. And I think the rebrand helped everyone from the acquired companies turn the corner to become one company, with one integrated offering, and one culture.

But even with that rebrand, I still sense that you don't feel great about the integration.

Before I left, I was leading the systems integration project for all of LRW/ Material. The CEO told me, "Hey, you're the only person with systems integration experience. Can you do this project to integrate—to select a new best in breed set of platforms and then migrate all of these companies to this new platform?" So we hired a big management consulting firm. They did a whole systems strategy and selected Workday and Salesforce. And it changed the way that everyone across the entire workflow worked, from sales to delivery, to finance, everything. And if that's not done well, you change the way people work. You make their jobs harder and worse, and all of a sudden the morale is just tanking. When we integrated the systems, it changed little things, like how we invoice those legacy clients. The client's like, "Well, I like the way that we were doing it before."

I don't know how to get around that. Because if that company is going to try and maximize their value, maybe go to market and have another private equity event, they can't sell that company with 12 different financial systems, 12 CRM systems. So it's a necessary evil. You can't overlook the impact that it's going to have on everybody, and process, and the culture.

Let's talk about the work and clients. Were the teams able to do better and more impactful work, or work with different clients?

Synergies played a big part of the deal conversation. I truly believe the thesis behind the acquisitions, and the intention to provide top quality creative services from research through design and build, is a good one. And I'm confident that over time, if they haven't already, Material will realize that value, own a differentiated and valuable place in the market, and deliver a ton of value to clients.

But it's going to take hard work, dedication and time. As an example, after the acquisition, we looked at their pipeline and their existing accounts, and they looked at ours. We said, "Oh gosh, you guys are in some big clients that T3 would like to work with. We're going to start selling these." So after the transaction, we started joint account planning sessions. The problem we ran into is the buyers that LRW was selling to were very different from the buyers that we were selling to. In fact, in most cases, they were in a very different part of the organization.

Right before I left, we sold a large digital transformation deal. It came through one of LRW's relationships. We said, "Great, T3 can do digital transformation. So pitch them digital transformation." And we incorporated research into the proposal. But research for us means we're going to go do a couple ride-alongs and some contextual inquiry, stuff like that. LRW would do hardcore survey-based quant research. They said, "This is how we do it. We need this much time to do it." We said, "No, no, we're starting the design process there." So it became a bit of a challenge.

And that conflict extended into who owns the client, who talks to the client, all the little petty things, as well as how the work gets done.

We had these two teams coming together, and there wasn't any trust between those two teams yet. So every little thing became an escalation.

It was really, really simple stuff, which should be easy to have a conversation about, but that speaks to the cultural clash and the lack of trust because we hadn't worked together before. So everything became this fire: blow up, come back, blow up, come back, blow up. They said that we're not using the insights coming out of the research. Blow up, come back. We said that those insights don't inform digital transformation. Blow up, come back. It was a big and important learning process for us all.

I can imagine that would drive you crazy.

Completely. All of those extra conversations are taking away from what we want to do, which is do the work... just do great work. So now you're spending 40% of your time on deescalations and education and collaboration with the internal team, as opposed to spending time with the client or advancing the work.

What are some things that you think you could have done differently to have the deal go smoother?

It's all about culture and communication. You have to be purposeful about the culture and either make the transaction a cultural addition or make it purposefully separate.

On the communication side, we could have brought the team in earlier to let them know what was happening, to bring them into the process and have more time to digest what was about to happen—to get mentally and emotionally prepared. I recognize there are downsides to that, too; taking the eye off the ball of our current book of business could have been disruptive to the transaction itself. So I realize that that isn't as easy as it sounds either.

On the culture side, being purposeful about the duration of keeping companies and teams separate, vs integrating immediately. Having a more thought-through integration plan, as opposed to just saying, "Okay, we're going to bring these companies together. We're going to start working together." I should have figured out some of the things that I mentioned earlier around titles and leveling and equity, and made those moves first. It was super disruptive, but unavoidable.

But I don't think it's all bad. A lot of what I shared with you sounds like negative learnings, but I don't think an entrepreneur's experience selling their design firm has to be negative. I think you need to figure out why you are selling, and that needs to be part of your pitch. If it's a good design firm, it's going to be wildly valuable, and so I would say, don't settle for any reason. And if the founder is like, "I've had it and I'm done," or "I just don't want to do the finance and the sales stuff," that should inform which buyer to go with. What's the right fit for your buyer?

You need to be really honest with yourself about why you're selling, and then stand firm when you get all these offers to make sure that the offer is one that will live up to what is important to your team and your legacy.

The Roadshow

Some of the leaders I spoke with had a single buyer in mind, or were approached by one or two companies. Christian described a different process (sometimes literally called "a process," as in "I'm going through a process,") one where T3 explored relationships with a variety of companies prior to selecting a potential buyer; he explained that he met with 12 different companies!

This process is almost always orchestrated by a banker (or M&A advisor). They have a network of potential buyers, they understand the temperature of the market, and they know exactly how to run the process. The process is a bit of a roadshow, and sometimes it's even referred to that way. I talked previously about the process of generating the preliminary financial model, sending out the teaser, and then sharing the Confidential Information Memorandum (or CIM). This is the result of that process: meeting with candidate buyers.

This is a part of the process where we as consultants excel. It's a storytelling activity, one where you paint a picture of a compelling, persuasive, and exciting future. It's just like a business development activity, where you hope to learn and sell simultaneously. The fundamentals of business development apply, like speaking with confidence and clarity, quickly building rapport, learning about what your audience wants to see before diving in, and checking in to make sure people are tracking. No need to go into detail on those here— you're probably already an expert! But there are some things you'll encounter that are slightly different than your typical business development or client-engagement call.

Showing your finances

A big part of these meetings are focused on the fundamentals of your business: your financial health and forecast. You'll be asked to describe the clients you have and industries they are in, their relative proportion to your overall revenue, your history with them, and your projection of work you'll bring in from them in the future.

Many smaller consultancies have established themselves with the support of one or two anchor clients—big companies that have trusted them with large, ongoing and dependable work. You'll hear later from Max Burton, who developed a very strong relationship with Carnival Cruise Company, and Crystal Rutland, who ultimately sold her company to one of her big clients, and we've already heard from Maria, who mentioned that Facebook was one of her existing clients. But while these large clients help a new company get established, they present worry to a buyer; too much consolidation around a single client rests an awful lot of risk on one set of shoulders. Anticipate questions about this form of consolidation, and if you have it, how you intend to diffuse it.

Additionally, you'll be asked about the projections you've developed in your financial models that were summarized in your CIM and that have been socialized by your banker. This is where you'll field questions about your assumptions. If you indicated 50% year-over-year growth for the next three years, what are you basing that on? A buyer's looking for plausibility.

You'll also get questions about how you generate business. This is an indicator of how quickly you can scale your revenue. Do you have a sales machine in place, or are you personally selling all the work? Are prospects coming to you, or are you out there hustling? What investment will the company need to put into your business to help you achieve your growth plans?

Showing your work

A fundamental part of a creative services company is, clearly, the creativity: what gets made, how it gets made, and why it's valuable. We never pitch work or engage with a client without something to show and to visually respond to. We were surprised, then, to find out that showing a case study or diving into a work sample wasn't a typical part of the initial roadshow meeting. It wasn't discouraged, but it also wasn't part of what's normal. Instead, it seems much more typical to *talk* about the work and working process, but spend more time focusing on clients, the financials, sales pipeline development, and the mechanics of profitability.

That makes sense, given that these meetings are often orchestrated by bankers or private equity companies; a financial focus is literally their job and what they care about the most.

But visual assets, artifacts and stories, are our industries' primary means of speaking, and without them, we're not showing as best as we can. If these meetings aren't being organized around a short case study of what you do, how you do it, and the value you provide, push back and make sure you are driving a part of the agenda.

Taking up your time and energy

Imagine Christian's experience: exploring a relationship with 12 different companies. Being conservative, that's 12 one-hour prep sessions, 12 one-hour meetings, 12 one-hour debriefs, 5–10 hours of scheduling, 30 days of travel, and a flurry of emails: a floor of 100 hours, and likely a lot more. And that's just the first round of dating! After all of those meetings, you can expect a subset to move to a next set of conversations, and those may be much longer and in more depth. All-in-all, if you're taking the company on a roadshow, mentally prepare for up to a month of solid meetings, and for hearing yourself talk about and hype your company over, and over, and over.

While you're doing this, you won't be running your business—at least not as effectively as you're used to. Get a plan in place for who is going to handle all of the things you normally do. You'll probably have to tell these people why you'll need extra help, and so this is a place where having a partner or close confidant within the company becomes helpful.

Conversations

Sue and Alan Cooper, Who Founded Cooper and Then Sold It to Wipro/Designit in October 2017

Sue and Alan Cooper need little introduction, as the Cooper name has been a rock in the history of interaction design. Their company, first named Cooper Software and then simply Cooper, was founded in 1992. The pair grew the studio in size and reputation, wrote and published books, and created Cooper U, a dedicated educational arm of the company. They sold the company in 2017, and now they run a ranch.

Why did you both start Cooper?

Alan: Because I couldn't get a job (laughs).

Sue: He couldn't get a job. And then I stepped in, "Okay, well, I guess we're going to have to do this on our own." Alan had this passion for separating design from building it. He hung his shingle out saying, "I'm going to do this consulting thing for design consulting, no programming," and got three clients right away. So then I was the back end and making sure that we were set up as a business and getting the contracts done. And then it naturally evolved and we hired our first employee and he came to the house and I went, "Shit, we've got to get an office."

This was back in 1992, and I felt like people were burning out in Silicon Valley, and I wanted to have a company where we didn't burn out people. There was Alan's passion to design and make, just create stuff that doesn't frustrate people so much. So then we had to write the books. We knew that consulting, books, and teaching all went together. And so we started Cooper U and did all of the wonderful things that had to happen in order to have a viable business.

We grew to about 70 people.

And I think about 10 years in, we were approached by a company who wanted to buy us, right before the dot com bust (2000), but we weren't ready. We didn't have an investment banker or anything. So one of the key stories for me is that I often look back to what they were offering then—and we could have sold out then for probably more than we eventually got—but we didn't feel ready. We just weren't ready to talk to them, we weren't ready to sell. We had too much to do. And then boom, the dot com crash happened so it's probably good we didn't sell because—

Alan: We would've gotten a lot of worthless stock. We would've gotten a much bigger number that was not backed by real money, I think. The dot com bubble popped and we just got destroyed, so we dropped down. Sue took over because I couldn't handle it, I was losing my shit. And Sue came in and basically rescued the company and she pared it down to, I think there were 7 people, 7 employees besides us.

Sue: By 2015 or 2016, I had grown the company back. Alan was off having fun. And I wanted to have fun, too. So I hired a company to help sell Cooper—an investment firm that didn't have any experience in our area, but they were really good salespeople. I hadn't done any research. I hadn't asked anybody else. Adaptive Path had just been purchased, and I should have asked them; I should have asked around. But I ended up interviewing all these investment bankers, and this one company that we hired was absolutely a disaster, they hadn't done any deals in our area. They didn't know the segment, they didn't understand the value of design.

It helped us realize what we needed to do to get ready for another investment banking firm. We had to get our marketing together to make Cooper a valued name brand. We had to communicate our messages more clearly so that an investment banker-type would be able to understand it.

I had to get our revenue up after this failed investment banking thing. I decided to hire a consultant, Ken Trush out of New York; Maria Giudice recommended him.

Ken told us, "In order to be attractive, you really need to have a broader reach and an executive team in place that is a little stronger than what you have." So we acquired a design company called Catalyst based in New York. Their company had about 15 people. The merger gave us a New York office in addition to our 45-person San Francisco office.

I knew that we had done the right thing with Catalyst when Nick (Gould, President of Catalyst) and his team of 15 people made baseball cards to introduce themselves to our team. Each baseball card had a picture of the person and their stats. It was such a great thing to do because you're meeting so many people at once that you need a little cheat sheet. I thought that was brilliant.

Alan: I actually think the Catalyst and Cooper merger illustrates a key point. In order for any kind of a merger or acquisition to be a success, the two companies involved have to be the same size. The closer to the same size they are, the better the chances are for a successful integration. We were three times bigger in terms of personnel. But we were a small single office shop and they were a small single office shop, and we're running the way a small company runs, not the way a big company runs. We don't think in terms of multimillion-dollar deals. We were thinking in terms of $100,000 deals. And we stressed from the very beginning that we were not acquiring Catalyst, we were merging with them. And that's, let me just say, that kind of humility is not to be found when a big company buys a little company.

Sue: One of the most important keys to our successful sale was retaining the right person to help. Luckily, we met Julie Levenson at La Honda Advisors in Palo Alto. She was like the calm center of the storm during the entire acquisition process, and much of our success was due to her expertise.

So you had established a joint company that was bigger and more attractive to buyers, and had successfully merged with Catalyst. Then what happened?

Sue: This company Wipro approached us. And we said, "Yeah, we'd like to talk."

Wipro had acquired Designit, a European firm quite large for an interaction design consultancy. They had the lead. So our firm would become part of Designit, which was part of Wipro.

Alan and I knew we wanted out. We didn't want to be part of the buyout terms. So we kept out of the inner workings of the deal negotiations because we wanted to show that our company can stand on its own without us there. Nick became the key Cooper lead for our sale. He carried the ball all the way to the finish line.

Were there retention milestones built into the deal as well?

Alan: It was a remarkable and unexpected thing—Wipro basically said from the beginning that the Coopers are out. They held me to a three-year commitment to come at their beck and call. They could say, "We need Alan Cooper here now," and I had to show up. They never once asked me.

We also had a non-compete for three years, too, not to work with other firms or whatever. But now I could start a new UX design company if I like.

Sue: Go for it, honey (laughs).

Why do you think Wipro felt so strongly about the two of you not staying on?

Sue: I think it was because they recently had a bad experience with a company they acquired, where the founders were a pain in the ass. They didn't want to see their methods and all this stuff change. You have to let the new company take on its new part, and they thought if we were there, we would've probably fought them a little bit more.

Tell me a little about the negotiation process.

Alan: Wipro had 5,000 employees, and we had 50. The way I think about it is that in an acquisition situation, especially when you've got different size companies, the negotiations are like a ratchet joint. It's a joint that spins one way. And it always spins against the little company.

Early on in the negotiations, they come in and they say, "Oh, we want to buy you. This is going to be a match made in heaven. Everything is wonderful. Here's the amount of money we're going to give you." And you say yes. And then they say, "Okay, we need to look a little closer." And they look a little closer and they go, "Well, we've got to give you a little less money." And again, they look a little closer, and say, "We've got to give you a little less money," and then a little less money.

And in the meantime, you're getting more and more committed to this. You're a little tiny company. They have 50 people on their M&A team; you have 50 people in your whole company.

And so then you finally consummate the deal and at the last minute they say, "Well, of course you're responsible for these taxes," which nobody ever mentioned. And so you just have to write a check for $300,000 or $400,000. It comes out of your pocket. And then they say, "Oh, by the way, didn't we mention that there's this other thing that you have to pay for?" And then there's this fee to these lawyers, and then there's this thing and that thing.

And so there's this constant ratcheting of things that you have to give, but the initial price that you agreed on, that never changes. Once you sign the deal, the money they give you, that's a number that's written down. The things that you're giving them, all of a sudden they're kind of fluid and they're constantly changing and they always change in one direction. They never come in and say, "Oh, by the way, we picked up the tab for this thing, for travel, for negotiations." And instead they say, "Oh no, that's on you."

Believe it or not, Sue finally settled this thing just a couple of months ago. Keep in mind, we sold the company five years ago. We had an office in California and we had an office in New York State. And so even though we're a tiny little company, and the amount of money we sold it for is just down in the rounding errors of the state revenues, we're a soft target. They don't come after Wipro, the giant multinational corporation with huge deep pockets; they come after tiny little Cooper. California wanted us to pay taxes on that transaction, and

New York wanted us to pay taxes on that transaction. Well, you don't have to pay taxes in two different states, but it's going to cost you five years and several hundred thousand dollars in legal fees just to straighten that mess out.

Sue: New York decided to audit us because they thought that more of our revenue was produced out of New York than California, so they didn't think they got their fair share. We had to go back into history and prove it to them. But they ended up deciding that New York was owed more anyway. So we had to pay New York more. You can get that money back from California, but it took several years to negotiate it back.

It's actually in our favor because California taxes are higher than New York. We weren't cheating or anything, it's just New York wanted to get their claws in for more money.

These deals have a long tail. You think you're done, and then these unexpected little things come up.

I sense you have a different sentiment between your merger with Catalyst and your sale to Wipro.

Alan: When we acquired Catalyst, it was really a merger of equals. And we very much wanted a win-win. We wanted them to be successful. We wanted to create a New York office and we wanted to learn from them and we wanted them to learn from us, and they wanted the same thing and it worked really well. We're not business executives, we're entrepreneurs and we're driven not by making money, we're driven by doing good work and that's a very different thing.

But once a company passes 100 or 150 people, it kind of stops doing that. You get professional management in, and their job is to make money and they don't care about win-win. They care about winning and that's a very different thing.

The problem is that the big companies want to buy you because they can't re-create what you do inside their organization. The reason why they can't re-create what you do inside their organization is because of their culture. The large size of the business says that whenever we have options, we always take the one that brings the biggest yield. Well, the one that always brings the biggest yield is the one that is proven. The bean counters never opt for the risky acquisition. And mergers and acquisitions people, they're bean counters to the nth degree. They're the beaniest of bean counters.

When the acquisition is completed, your organization is now in the bloodstream of a larger company that has antibodies against who you are and what you do.

And in my humble opinion, there are very few acquisitions that actually work.

The Wipro guys wanted the Cooper people to behave like Wipro employees. The Wipro employees work differently and think differently. And our guys said, "No, that's not how we do things, and the reason why we're successful at what we do is because of the way we do things." And the management up and down in Wipro, they were just unsympathetic to that. They said, "No, no, no, you can do your magic, but you have to do it our way." Well, that's just a way of saying, "We're going to destroy you and everything you stand for."

When their bean counters were counting and evaluating your company, did you speak with other potential buyers?

Sue: No. The biggest gotcha was that Wipro didn't want us talking to other firms, they wanted to tie us up, because they said, "We're going to put a lot of time and energy into this deal and we want you to not talk to anybody else."

And so we agreed to that, stupidly, and then we were waiting, waiting, waiting. I think the hardest part for me was waiting for them because they just dragged it out so long. It's a big company and they need to do their machinations, but then we couldn't talk to anybody else. So now we're tied up, can't talk to anybody else, and are committed to this deal.

It was a mistake to agree to not talk to anybody else because we lost any sort of leverage that we had at that point.

It's a tiny deal, and they're working on huge deals and this is just this little one. And the little one can take as much time and resources as this big giant deal.

Where was your anxiety level during all of this?

Sue: Oh God, it was horrible. Nick handled it all, and I didn't want to call him every day, "What's happening? What's happening?" So I would just try not to call him.

It was really hard to keep people at the time. There were a lot of other companies poaching our people. With every person who leaves, your value goes down because they look at how many people you have. And so that was stressful.

Then we went into a little bit of a hiccup in the economy back five, six years ago. That was stressful because our revenue wasn't meeting the projected revenue that we had given them.

We were waiting, just waiting. Having the ball in their court was so frustrating, because you're just sitting there going, "Okay, I guess we'll just continue doing business and do the best we can."

Eventually, the deal closed, and Cooper became part of Designit and Wipro. You stepped back from the company, but you certainly got to watch it from afar. How did you feel about what you saw?

Sue: When we acquired Catalyst, we were very careful to honor their culture and they were very careful to honor ours. So it was a much more simpatico kind of situation. They were very respectful, and Cooper's culture was to kick ass and take names and we're going to show you how to do this. We have a special way of doing things.

And the Wipro Designit people didn't appreciate that. I kind of sensed that they respected Cooper and our reputation and the books and the methodology and all that, but that they were thinking, "That's fine, we know that stuff and we're going to do it our way."

Alan: At the last minute they decided to change our name from Cooper to Designit, which is a grossly bad business decision.

Sue: But that's their right. They bought the company, they bought the rights to do that, and if they don't see leverage in the name, then they need to do what they're going to do.

Alan: I'm not saying that they didn't have the right to do that. I'm saying that it was a grotesquely poor business decision. If you're selling your company, you've got to let go, and you can't run a company from the grave. You can't have these strings attached. They don't want it and you don't want it, and you don't want to be involved in that.

This is why you don't want to accept an earnout. If you accept an earnout as part of your compensation for an acquisition, what you're doing is you're saying, "My compensation will be for running the company the way I always run it, except I no longer have the control to run it that way." It's just a suicide pact. So you never ever want an earnout. An employment contract is okay. Even a modest non-compete is okay. But an earnout is ridiculous.

Sue: Because you're being measured on your success...

Alan: ...but you're not in control of your success.

Sue: You're not in control anymore. And as an entrepreneur we are used to having a lot of control.

We sold the Cooper name, the Cooper URL, everything. The Cooper website, it's gone. And so now there's no way to find any information about Cooper on the net. For people who are putting down Cooper as their resume, they can't find us anywhere. They can't find any information about the company.

There's absolutely no information about what we did. It's like we didn't exist, it's erased. And I wish there was a way, for our employees who are looking for jobs and as a service to ex-employees who want to stay in touch with each other or whatever... I think we should have thought that through a little bit better.

Are you glad you sold?

Sue: Oh, yeah. Yeah, I was done. It was time. There's no question for me.

We were in our sixties when we sold the business. When we were approached the first time we were in our forties and we were not ready for it. We had the energy to keep going. But it was really an easy decision for us the second time because we both wanted to retire. We were in our sixties, so that's a huge, huge part of the equation for me.

I like having a happy end to the story. It's nice to feel like I did something, that I set out to do something and we achieved it.

Alan: I think it's important to state that it's commonly accepted wisdom that you cannot sell a service company. Obviously service companies sell, but I think that the odds are against selling a service company. I think that also the odds are against a successful sale of a small company to a big company. Because the entrepreneurial mindset is very different from the corporate mindset. And so deals get made. We made a deal, you made a deal. And if you can make a deal, if you can sell your modestly sized consulting company, you are fucking awesome.

And you need to understand just how difficult that is, just how fraught that challenge is, and to understand that you've climbed the Everest of business accomplishment to do that. And you need to pat yourself on the back.

The Letter of Intent

As we saw earlier, your financial model led to a valuation which is based heavily on your revenue and a multiplier. It's also based on things like headcount, client base, and the goal of the acquisition (for example, Facebook was entirely uninterested in Maria's clients, but wanted to really understand the staff they would be hiring). When you've worked the roadshow and gotten some interest from potential buyers, you'll arrive at the Letter of Intent, or LOI, part of the process.

This is when things start to get and feel pretty real, and is really the main chance you have to negotiate for the things that matter to you: it's when you have a big opportunity to exercise your "walk away" leverage, because—while you've likely invested hours and hours in time so far—it's actually the least amount of effort you'll put into the process, compared to what comes next. If the buyer is serious about acquiring your company, this is your chance to both implicitly or explicitly threaten to abandon the deal.

What's in the LOI?

The letter of intent is a meaningful signal that a buyer is interested in a purchase, and is interested in a purchase at a certain price. It includes cash, but also all other parts of a deal.

For example, let's say you've built a business that generates $5 million in revenue, and you've been valued, at a 2x multiple, as having a $10 million dollar company. When the deal is done, you aren't going to have a $10 million dollar check in your pocket.

A typical package is likely to be built on a combination of cash, stock, retention, and incidentals. *Cash on close* is what most of us imagine when we think of selling our company, and it is almost always a substantial part of a deal. In our $10 million example, you may actually walk away with a check for $4 million in cash, and like Maria described, that feels pretty amazing!

So, what about the rest? It may be tied to some, or all, of these items:

- Equity (stock) in the buyer's company. If the acquiring company is a public company, you'll be able to easily map their (current) stock price to the number of shares you are being offered. You may be granted shares of stock at that price, but you don't get them all at once: they *vest* over a period of time, in chunks (often about ¼ per year). If the company *isn't* publicly traded, you'll have to think hard about the potential worth of that stock. Do you think the buyer will have an exit event—going public, or selling *themselves*? If not, you'll end up with some worthless paper.

- The retention of you. Depending on how "important" you are to the brand and the daily running of the company, you'll likely be financially motivated to stick around: often, you'll receive money if you stay one year, two years, and so-on. This one's a leap of faith, too. Maria left Facebook with a lot of money on the table, and you'll read about others doing the same, because they just couldn't handle the new company culture.

- The retention of your team members. A company may be interested in your staff, and so they'll commit to hiring a certain percentage or number of your designers. Your compensation will be tied to those numbers, although you may not have much control over your teams' willingness to stay after close.

- Hitting financial targets ("earning out" the rest of the money owed— what Alan Cooper advised to never sign up for). We'll talk much more about earnouts later in this book.

What happens if it isn't in the LOI?

The legal part of the process that follows a signed letter of intent will leave room for negotiating various parts of the deal. But a buyer will be highly reluctant to revisit and argue about the *financial* parts of the deal. And finances touch a lot of different parts of the agreement, not just the cash up front.

Simply, if it isn't in the LOI and it's related to money, it is going to be extremely hard to argue for later, and so you may end up in a situation where, like Gavin and Sue and Alan, you're taking someone on their word.

For example, let's say you want to work with your co-founders again after you leave the acquiring company. You may view this as a fairly simple point, but a buyer will see this as a point of leverage—fine, they may say, if you want the freedom to leave as a group, we'll need to minimize that risk by taking something away or including a penalty. If you wait to discuss this after you've signed an LOI, you are negotiating without much leverage, because you've all already agreed upon the value of the company and the transaction. Any penalty or takeaway is coming out of that agreed-upon value.

You'll have months and months to negotiate the details of the transaction, but before you sign the LOI, you have the most leverage and are the least emotionally invested. Explore this space as long as possible to make sure you get the most out of the details. I'll share more thoughts on this later in the Appendix.

Phil Barrett, Who, With His Wife Debre, Founded Flow Interactive's African Presence and Sold It to Deloitte in 2014

When Phil Barrett and his wife, Debre, moved to South Africa, they found a gap in the service market—very few companies were offering UX services. They started Flow Interactive's Africa office, and after growing it, they sold it to Deloitte Digital.

Phil, tell me a little about how you ended up in South Africa running a design studio.

Flow Interactive was started in the UK in about 1999 by Meriel Lenfestey. I came to join her, and we grew to about 45 people. My wife is from South Africa, and around 2006—we had a daughter who was three—my wife said, "London is no place to raise a child. Let's go to South Africa." And I thought, "Well, I guess I'll keep working remotely." But then Meriel let me borrow the brand; I paid her one pound for the brand, and started up in South Africa.

We offered good user experience design services: usability testing, user research, ethnography, diary studies, and interviews; and detailed interaction design for organizations.

We grew that to about 15 people, and then sold it to Deloitte.

Why did you start thinking about selling the company?

My wife, who was our COO, was getting very bored. I was also getting a bit bored. We reached a ceiling where we kept having the same clients, and the same conversations. Design is always ultimately limited by the choices that organizational leadership is making. You end up in the situation where, as a designer getting direction from your clients, you say, "Why the hell do they want us to do that?"

I had been doing design for about 15 years, and I said, "I know all of these patterns. Now I want to go and see why they happen." And I didn't quite have the vocabulary, or the contacts, or the skills, or the positioning, to know how to do that.

I wanted to get access to the boardroom to see who the hell was making these various decisions, and why they were making them. Why don't companies use design right? Why do companies make dumb decisions about the way they use design? I needed to break through to a different level to understand how those decisions were being made, and by whom, and what factors they were considering.

How did you end up speaking with Deloitte?

At the same time as I was feeling this frustration, it was an acquisition festival. The consultancies were all buying design shops; it was trendy. They were all buying design operations. We were getting a fair amount of interest; there were two consultancies who approached us, and one was Deloitte.

A contact of ours had gone to become a partner at Deloitte Digital, and he was the one who was driving Deloitte to think about acquiring us. He knew that we were a valuable asset, and that Deloitte had a gap, and he always admired the work that we did.

Deloitte was trying to invest in design. They were trying to build Deloitte Digital South Africa, and they were investing in acquiring all sorts of different bits and pieces to build. They were keen to acquire us, and we had somebody on the inside who was rooting for us all the way, and so the acquisition itself was not particularly difficult. I wasn't surprised about their interest in us. We were sure that we were damn good at what we did, and their interest in design—that was a trend that was happening. We could see the trend, and we were understanding that we were part of that trend.

The risk to them for the acquisition was pretty damn low, because it wouldn't take them long to earn back the money that they spent on the acquisition.

Because it's only a tiny acquisition, really, in the grand scheme of things. So it was a very low cost, or very low risk venture for them.

Were they only interested in the design talent, or also in your client base?

Oh, definitely the clients. We brought in about 20 million rand in existing contracts, which in those days would have been between $1 and $2 million US dollars. For Deloitte, especially in South Africa, they have many, many, many relationships, but they don't necessarily have opportunities to sell. So we brought new opportunities to make deals, which they could then use to expand, and keep extending their involvement.

Let's talk about the negotiation process. What was the structure of your compensation package?

There was a cash upfront payment, plus we were to pay out our cash reserve. We always used to run Flow in a very conservative way, with a very large cash reserve, because it just means you can sleep at night. If you don't have a large cash reserve, then you don't know if you're going to make payroll at any given point. So we used to run Flow with the big cash reserve, and that cash reserve would be paid out to us in cash payments up front.

And then there'd be an earnout period, which was based on performance. So if we sold a lot of business, we earned a lot of extra money, and if we didn't sell a lot of business, then we didn't earn a lot of extra money. There was a three year earnout period stipulated. But if you think about it, the earnout didn't really have teeth, because if they're saying, "Well, we'll pay you the money on a yearly basis as you earn it," you sell work, you make money, you take a proportion of that for yourself. Once that money's paid, it ain't getting paid back.

So if in year three you're like, "Eh, I don't want to do this anymore," they're like, "Fine."

We also had conversations and negotiations around office space. Part of the recipe for happy, happy, happy designers is an environment that the designers enjoy being in. We went to the Deloitte offices in downtown Cape Town, and they're in a nice location, but the offices themselves were incredibly awful. It was designed by accountants for accountants, or by consultants for consultants. So just nasty everything, nasty plastic desks, low ceilings, bad lighting, just an utterly joyless environment in every conceivable way. We said, "Deloitte Digital needs to be a bright, happy, exciting, funky, modern, joyful, true-to-materials, livable space." And Deloitte demonstrated good faith there, because I think they believed in that as well, as best they could. So there were some constraints on what they could and couldn't do, but they understood that Deloitte Digital needed to be a different beast from Deloitte Consulting, because it was a different pitch to the market, and a different ethos, and a modernization of their brand and so on.

There was also some negotiation about usability labs, because usability labs at that time were very important. These days, usability testing is mostly done via Zoom, so the concept of the lab is much less of a thing anymore. But in those days, usability labs were key. We'd have real fleshy humans wheeled in and we would test things on them.

And we also discussed workshop spaces. If you're trying to have a fun and engaging workshop with clients, and you bring them into a sad gray room with no windows and dingy lighting, it's not good. So there was a special lab and workshop space, which was part of the setup. They did their very best on that, as well.

Were the things related to the office space in writing—in the actual sale contract?

No, I don't think so. The intention was so visible that it never crossed our mind to do that. There was enthusiasm on both sides to do this thing, and Deloitte was genuinely committed to it. One of the things that Deloitte has worldwide is this concept of the Deloitte Greenhouse, which is ideation spaces, big expensive ideation spaces that they rent out to clients for days, or a week, or whatever. And it's part of their recipe. So they looked at our requests for improved spaces and they were like, "Oh, that's nothing. You should see what we've got." And they took us on a tour of their Johannesburg Greenhouse and said, "And we're building one of these in Cape Town as well," which they were. So we were quite convinced that they understood the value of creating interesting spaces.

So how did it work out?

There are different kinds of acquisition, as I understand the landscape. There are companies like WPP who buy agencies and leave those agencies to operate. They try not to mess with the secret sauce; they just accumulate many, many agencies. Each agency has its own special recipe, and they try to extend those, and harvest the cash, and so on. Whereas Deloitte was about acquiring and digesting. The other company goes away and the staff become Deloitte Digital.

After the acquisition, I found myself as an Associate Director, which is one level down from a Director, which is a Partner. As an Associate Director, I was just a senior salaried employee. And I had that earnout I described before... I thought I had a two-year earnout clause, but it turned out I had a three year. It said in the contract, your presence is material to the value of this contract, etc. etc. And then at the beginning of year three, I thought, "I've done my two year earnout and there's an opportunity that's come up at Absa Bank, so I think I'll go for it." I went to them and I'm like, "Cool, so I'm going to quit and start working at Absa Bank." And they're like, "What do you mean? You've still got another year to go." I said, "Oh, but I don't want to." And they had no actual hold over me at that point.

The whole venture was not generating much of a profit.

Uh oh.

At first, nothing changed. We started off in our office while they were building out the office space at Deloitte. Then there was induction (laughs).

Deloitte is very, very entrepreneurial. There's a central set of services, and you can make use of those services, but then the cost of those services is deducted from your P&L. They told me, "Yes, you can send all the employees on induction. It's mandatory."

We said, "But we don't want to spend all this money. It seems terribly expensive. Can't you just induct us for free?"

They said, "No."

And we said, "Well, we don't really want to pay."

They responded that "It's okay. It's only mandatory."

We said, "I thought mandatory meant that you had to do it."

And then they said, "No, no, that's compulsory."

So we skipped it. I think what we did is we sent one guy on induction and he said it was the most godawful, meaningless week of his life; we thought we wouldn't do any more of that.

There were all the Associate Director's dinners and shindigs. My wife and I were invited to a dinner to celebrate the deal. We flew off to Johannesburg and we sat around the table and had dinner and drank champagne. My wife was already becoming fairly convinced these were not "her people." Her approach was, "I'll put up with this for a couple of years so we can finish the deal."

She slowly uncovered the spectacular degree of sexism that existed within the organization. It was casual sexism. It wasn't ill-intended... it was just thoughtless, unconsidered, old school, traditional sexism. They just hadn't really thought about it. It was a man's world.

I've got a higher tolerance for "not our people" than she has. But also I was not subjected to the sexism that she was, so it was easier for me. So I just tried to do business with them.

Perhaps it's an understatement, but it doesn't sound like it was a great fit.

I was excited about the money. I was bored of running the old organization. I figured I could handle whatever bullshit the next couple of years would bring, and that it probably would be a good learning opportunity. So I was mostly happy. Happy is a strong word. I was mostly able to cope with it.

But by the end of the two and a half years I was ready to go.

We marveled at the incredible inefficiency and illogical corporate silliness that we encountered. We knew that organizations could be pretty dumb, because we'd had plenty of big organizations as clients. But actually being inside one and witnessing the madness from the inside, it was definitely quite something to behold...

It was bureaucracy, old-school bureaucracy. All of the archaic SAP systems, and spreadsheets, and so on.

We brought Slack with us and we tried to get Deloitte Digital to accept Slack. All of the people who were from other parts of Deloitte Consulting burned out on Slack almost immediately. They just couldn't understand how it worked; I found out that the Managing Director was trying to read every single message in the whole of every channel on Slack, which was why he thought it was impractical.

They had their old-school software tools. Just trying to log your expenses required an extensive training course and a lot of luck.

If you say to a designer, "Cool, well, I know you've just been on this trip to Johannesburg to see this customer, so now you need to log your expenses. And to do that, you have to dial in through a VPN, and then you have to use this arcane tool, which doesn't really work on Safari or Chrome for Mac. And you have to know all of these extraordinary codes." I don't know, what's the code for a glass of wine? And then if you do it wrong, then it's like, "No, wrong, I'm not paying your expenses. Try again next month." And so that kind of thing doesn't make designers very happy.

Designers want the world to be a better place, and UX designers hate systems that are poorly designed, and the details matter to UX designers (which is why they're UX designers). And so every time you make them use a system which is poorly designed to do a task which is tangential to the thing they like doing, which is design, then they get pretty flipping annoyed. And it doesn't take much.

In fact, because of the systems being so difficult to use, and so not pleasant for designers, and then having a real impact on morale, we did the same thing that most people in Deloitte seemed to do, which was we hired an extra human whose job it was to use those systems. So we actually put an additional layer of abstraction on top of the systems by hiring Cindy, who was lovely and seemed to thrive on integrating herself with SAP and other things. The designers would fill in a simple form that said what their expenses were, and they would give it to Cindy, and Cindy would do the job for them. Which ate into the profits a little bit, but not that much.

Another thing that was "highly entertaining" was e-learning. Because Deloitte does a lot of work with banks, all Deloitte employees had to be compliant with certain regulations related to anti-money laundering, bribery, and corruption, that sort of thing. And so they had a mandatory, and by that I mean compulsory, process where Deloitte employees had to do e-learning modules to make sure that they understood about ethics and technicalities associated with above-board operation.

The e-learning was unspeakably bad videos and just dreadful things that you had to sit through hour after hour, clicking next, next, next, and it felt like an enormous waste of time.

In game testing, you can get bits of software that automatically click on various parts of the screen according to rules. So we set up a clicker to click on the next button every minute, and then we let it run overnight. Because you couldn't click next too fast, because it had timers on everything to make sure that you attended sensibly to each piece of content. So we set it to click next every minute, two minutes or whatever it was, and they just let it run overnight very, very slowly to get to the end of the e-learning.

We tried to cheer up the designers who had to sit through it by saying, "Oh, as part of your initial induction, you had to do a lot of e-learning." And so we bought a large Mexican sombrero and a lot of chocolate. When you were joining Deloitte Digital as a designer, and you had to do your e-learning stuff, you got to wear the sombrero of happiness and receive large amounts of chocolate.

It seems like the culture wasn't a match. What about the business itself?

People will pay a certain amount for design, people will pay a different amount for strategy consulting, or auditing, or so on. But Deloitte wanted to have a single rate card, and so they wanted us to sell design services at the same price as you'd sell C-level strategy, and auditing, and whatever.

It was very hard to sell. But part of the reason why you needed to charge so much was because the overheads were very high. In the P&L you're running, you have to pay lots of fees to other parts of the business for use of central admin services, e-learning, and whatever else. That pushes your fees up. So we were paying costs for things that we didn't value, and being told to put our fees up and make a certain amount of margin. In fact, there were complex margin calculator spreadsheets that you were supposed to use in order to work out what you could and couldn't charge for any given thing. And they were wildly arcane. Because it was basically an organization fundamentally founded by accountants. So the way that everything worked was in a very accountanty kind of way.

If you actually think about it and ask, "What's the matter here?" The matter is, if you've got an organization created by accountants, for accountants, operated by accountants, and you take those systems and try to apply them to design, they don't work very well. That's the truth of it.

The rate increase was astronomical. I don't know, I feel like it could have been a doubling or a tripling of our rates. Our rich clients, which would be the banks and the insurance companies, could still usually carry on paying. The rich clients could afford it, and the poor clients couldn't.

This wasn't malicious on Deloitte's part. They didn't know. They simply just had no idea. They'd never sold design in their lives before, and they didn't know what fees could or could not be commanded for design. They assumed that the Deloitte badge would easily open a whole bunch of new doors to new opportunities within clients for us, where we could charge all sorts of fabulous money. And there were some situations in which that was true, but not many.

Deloitte has lots of different units. You might have a strategy unit, and then the Deloitte Digital Software Development Team, and the Deloitte Digital Experience Design Team, which was us. And then you might have the salesforce.com experts and all these different units, each of whom has their own P&L, their own accounts. And then you'd have the Partners, the Senior Directors, who would be pulling together a pitch and would want to sell something wondrous to a big client.

They would ask for services from all these different units and say, "Okay guys, I think there's an opportunity to sell some UX. It'll make us look really good. Can you guys bid for this UX, or tell us how we should bid for this UX component of the job, or where we can put design into the job?" You would participate in those bids and occasionally, very occasionally, they would come off. Otherwise, you'd be selling your own work. And so you'd get credit for selling your own work, because you sold it and you billed for it, and it appeared on your accounts, and at the end of every quarter, you were supposed to be showing that you turned a profit for the business.

Are you glad you sold Flow Interactive and had this experience?

Have you ever read *Stumbling on Happiness*, by Daniel Gilbert?

No, I haven't.

It's truly a great book. Gilbert points out that the only way you can measure happiness is through self-report. The only way you can tell if somebody's happy is by asking them. And all the research into happiness shows that you can pretty much do whatever you like to a human, and provided they're still alive, if you ask them, "Are you pleased that such and such a thing happened?" they'll almost always say, "Yes."

They'll post-rationalize to identify that the thing that happened to them was for the best and that it was the course of life and so on. There are athletes who lost the use of their legs saying that it was the best thing that ever happened to them, that it was a really important change in their life.

So if you ask me, am I happy that it happened? My default answer as a human will be like, "It was the best thing. It was a real learning experience, and I'm sure that this was the true course of my life," and so on. And now here I am in my life in the Netherlands. Am I happy? I should be happy if I know what's good for me. Because I wasn't enjoying running the old company. We liberated a whole bunch of cash. I'm fucking lucky. The things I learned, and the things I witnessed were hilarious and fascinating, and I did learn things.

I learned that if you're sure that you want the money, and you are happy to let go of the asset, and you don't want the asset anymore... it's like, "I have had enough of running this fucking agency, I don't want to do it anymore, and I definitely am prepared to exchange all of that for some money and some heartache," then fine. But if secretly, actually, you love what you do, then chances are you'll sell it to somebody else who doesn't get it. Because almost by definition, if they're trying to buy it off you, they don't get it, because they couldn't do it themselves. And if you love what you do, then you probably should carry on doing what you love.

Retention Agreements & Earnouts

Phil described that he was tied to Deloitte for a period of time after his acquisition was finalized. Maria Giudice also described that a material amount of the money she made on the sale was contingent on her post-sale activities; Maria and a large portion of her team had to stay employed at Facebook for a specific amount of time, or she would forfeit cash (and she did!).

These types of requirements or, as they are sometimes called, *handcuffs*, are common in sale agreements. The reason is because, from the buyer's perspective, they are buying you: your ideas, your processes, your ability to lead, your tacit knowledge of the business, and your relationship with your clients and your team. If you leave, their acquisition becomes much riskier and, consequently, less valuable. Financial upside is a way to attract you to the deal. Retention agreements are a way to keep you after the deal is closed.

There are a few primary types of retention agreements that you may encounter. These typically tie money to *the amount of time you stay*, *the amount of revenue you bring in*, and *the amount of your team that sticks around.*

Money tied to the amount of time you stay

Often, an "earnout" is paid at the end of each year, over a period of time (typically 2–4 years). Sometimes that money is paid in progressively larger amounts, encouraging you to stay even after the initial glow of the deal wears off. Staying in a job feels pretty easy in the theoretical, but then the specifics kick in, which will try your patience:

- Maria was marginalized, stuck in a Director role, and ran into a culture clash that was insurmountable for her to manage
- Gavin found himself encountering corporate financial constraints he didn't expect
- Phil's wife Debre experienced an abusive environment

- Christian became responsible for internal IT system rollouts that were culturally contentious (and boring!)

In normal situations, you might quit jobs like these right away. But if millions are on the table, you might change your mind, even if you aren't happy. There's no way you can predict the future, but you can do your own cultural diligence by spending as much time as you can with the potential buyer before agreeing to terms. Can you find out the real gossip and real cultural highs and lows? Can you make an objective decision, rather than an emotional one, about how you may respond to this form of agreement?

Money tied to the amount of revenue you generate

The most typical form of retention agreement is based on your ability to keep doing what you were doing before—making money selling creative services. You would think that this is pretty clear; when you sign a new contract, the amount of the contract is added to your running revenue tally, and at the end of the retention term, you either made it or you didn't. But there are intricacies to revenue generation to consider.

In your agency—particularly if it was small—it was probably very clear who closed a deal. In fact, for some of the people I spoke with, they were the only ones selling, so it was very black and white. But larger deals in larger organizations have many people participating in the business development process. Phil described a complex formula used to identify how signed revenue was allocated to the sales team. Things become subjective, quickly.

Revenue recognition also gets more complicated to track and manage, because you'll lose visibility into the financial processes of a large organization. It's rare that your acquirer will work on a cash basis, but if they do, you may not have any view into accounts receivable for some time, because you aren't the one depositing the check anymore!

And we've all experienced the end-of-year crunch, when use-it-or-lose-it money becomes available from clients, but revenue targets loom. If you understand how you're tracking to a target, you might find some new enthusiasm to go the extra mile in a sale. But if the tracking is delayed, and you won't know where you stand until March or April of next year, it will become a shot in the dark.

Money tied to the amount of your team that sticks around

In an acqui-hire, the value of your company is in the people, and if the people leave, there would have been no reason for the buyer to buy the company in the first place. It would be advantageous to them to give you ways to encourage your team to stay, like discretionary funds for bonuses or cool pro-bono projects to work on. But it's rare that the buyer will do that, because they'll expect you to already have a strong relationship and rapport with your team.

If you tie your personal sale rewards to the retention of your team, you'll need to be really confident that you can keep people happy and challenged. One way to do this is to negotiate for a management carveout—to pass down the retention/reward to your team, and tie *their* bonuses to retention. But designers aren't always financially motivated, and so you may find yourself with few levers to pull when your team begins shying away from a new corporate culture or new types of project work. And that carveout may come out of your share of the money, meaning your overall take-home is materially less than you thought.

Playing out the doom and gloom

The situations above seem bleak. When you are negotiating any of these retention agreements, it becomes important to play out the following potential "what-if" scenarios in very clear, crisp and detailed language in your contract. These are real possibilities; as I spoke with founders, I heard stories about every single one of these examples. Give these scenarios real attention and contemplation, and then have your lawyer add explicit language to your contract related to each one.

What if you are fired with cause before your retention agreement is over?

"Cause" can be complicated, but imagine that you do something wrong—either something clearly indicative of poor judgment and incompetence, or something that can be described as poor performance. Do you get your earnout? What if you are in the process of being terminated, perhaps through a performance plan to be "managed out" when your earnout time period is up? Can they claw the money back after you've been let go?

What if you are fired without cause (perhaps through a layoff or reorganization)?

Large companies make changes all the time. What if the company makes a change that cuts your team, or you? Does this accelerate your earnout, or does the money disappear? Is it prorated based on when that layoff happens?

What if you are moved into a role that isn't a fit? What if you are marginalized, either on purpose or by mistake? And what if you get a new boss who sucks?

There are lots of passive-aggressive ways to kick someone out of an organization without firing them. In the movie Office Space, Milton is moved into the basement, without his red stapler. You'll hear later from Max Burton that, after selling his company Matter to Accenture, he suddenly found himself flying 100,000 miles each year to make his earnout numbers. Would that be enough for you to leave? And if you do, will you be walking away from your earnout?

What if you disagree with how revenue recognition is allocated?

If your money is tied to your ability to sell and close deals, a large amount of subjectivity is introduced into the process. I spoke with someone who sold his company to a very large IT integrator. After the sale, he would be brought into a large business development opportunity to run a creative workshop, get the potential client excited, and help them see the power of innovation and creativity. The multimillion-dollar sale would close, and he would be given credit for a tiny, tiny fraction of the deal's revenue, because it was perceived that he worked less on the deal. Is that fair? And if not, what's your ability to challenge the allocation?

A big challenge around revenue recognition comes at the end of the year. Imagine it's December and you have a target to hit by the end of the fiscal year. You deliver on the 15th of the month, everyone goes on vacation, and in the new year, you make some small changes at the request of the client. Can you recognize the revenue tied to that deliverable? What if your earnout is really close, and that deal will kick you over the edge?

What if your team is fired?

Imagine that your earnout is tied to retention of your team; a percentage of the team needs to stay for a certain amount of time. What happens if the company decides to do a round of layoffs? What if your new boss doesn't gel with some key members of the team?

Make it explicit

Each of these scenarios, while not likely, are also not impossible to imagine. The way to mitigate these is to answer the questions posed above, very explicitly, *in the contract*. Define what revenue recognition means and how it's calculated in excruciating detail. Work through what types of events accelerate your earnout, and pay particular attention to those events that are typical of larger companies (often related to layoffs, reorgs, and political infighting). Be sure you understand exactly what you have to do in order to make the money you've negotiated for. Don't take it for granted that everyone is using the same language and has the same understanding of the if/then terms. And most importantly, realize that anything and everything is negotiable. If your earnout feels tied to something out of your control, push back on it!

Matthew Robinson, Who Was Responsible for Integrating Idean Into Capgemini After It Was Acquired in 2017

I met Matthew when we both worked at frog. After his experience there, he joined Idean to run their Austin studio. Over time, his role expanded, and when Idean sold, he was put in charge of the integration. Later, Capgemini, the acquirer, went on to purchase frog, so somewhat ironically, Matthew found himself back where he started.

Matthew, tell me about your experience at Idean.

Idean was a global design research and design firm. It was founded in Finland, and was about a 23-year-old company when I left. Before the acquisition, we had about 200 designers in the United States, Finland, Germany, and the UK. After the acquisition, we had about 1,100 designers, with new offices in Norway, Sweden, and Shanghai.

I was with Idean for almost seven years. I was hired to run the Austin studio. I ended up then running the New York studio for a short time, as well. After the acquisition, I essentially ran North American operations and all integration activities, too.

How would you describe the company culture of Idean?

The company was about fun and making great things. That's a little bit of the ethos or tagline of most design firms, some flavor of that: love what you make; make great things... things like that. I didn't know much about Finnish culture before I started there, and I don't know if my founders were representative of the larger lot, but they were super fun guys, very gregarious.

That really percolated through the company. Our CEO and main founder was an incredibly gregarious guy, Risto Lähdesmäki. It was almost blasphemous at points, his energy and zeal for what we did. He founded this company with three or four of his colleagues in a room in Finland. It started from next to nothing; I think he was a keyboardist in a band when he decided to start the company.

I get together with former colleagues and employees a fair amount still, and we kind of kick ourselves now because I don't think we realized how good we had it. We didn't work crazy hours. I worked at frog before this, and it was a "crazy hour type of place" for the most part. I felt like Idean wasn't. They really protected everything. We priced all our projects based on an eight-hour day. And we'd get outside of that sometimes, but not often. It was a good community of people who we hired for culture. I know everybody says they do that, but I really felt like we stuck to our guns on that at Idean, and pretty much everybody got along very well, and it was a good place where people watched each other's backs.

How did financial operations happen at such a large scale?

Each studio had its own financials which rolled up to the country they were in, and that rolled up globally. I couldn't see all the way to net profitability of my studio just because a lot of our costs were globally shared, like software licenses, things like that. So it was kind of hard to slice things all the way down to that level. But I was responsible for my revenue target, as well as a margin target, as well as the utilization target for the people. Those were really our main metrics: we had an Austin target, a US target, and then global stuff that really only the C-level people paid attention to.

We met biweekly with all of the heads of studios across the globe and went over our numbers together. We were all in lockstep of how each studio was doing. So we could resource from a different studio if needed, if they needed help in hitting numbers and had utilization problems. We were pretty linked together.

Idean sold to Capgemini in 2020. Tell me about how the sale came about.

We actually weren't for sale. I don't know how the original conversation started, but at the same time, we got several unsolicited offers from several different companies, one of them being Capgemini. Capgemini was not the highest dollar amount. I don't think it wasn't even close. The highest dollar amount was from another large consultancy that has bought several design firms. The executive team didn't entertain any of them, except Capgemini, and the reason was because Capgemini had told us that they would leave us alone. They described that they had a hole in their business, and that they didn't do things the way we did. So they told us that they were willing to put into the acquisition agreement some kind of safeguards, to ensure we could continue to do what we did.

How much of that was lip service? I'm not sure. And in hindsight, some of it seemed like it was. Financials likely end up changing people's feelings about that eventually.

But since we weren't for sale, we said, "Okay, we'll do this. Here's our number. You have 30 days to do your due diligence." We had some leverage at the beginning.

I found out about the acquisition around day 15 of that 30 day diligence period. Leadership came to us and said, "Help us identify your key people who you want to make sure are retained, and taken care of, and they're happy through this thing," and started asking some opinions and questions on things at that point.

And when I found out, it felt good. The executives shared with us how it happened—that we weren't for sale, and that Capgemini said that we'll continue to do what we do. I think some people were a little more cautious and worried or nervous. Some of the management team had been there since closer to the beginning. People who had moved from Finland to the US in positions at about my level. But they were also in a better position to make some money, so I think overall everybody was happy. Just nobody really fully knew what to expect. But one thing we did know is nothing would actually change for a while, and that comforted everybody.

Why did you think nothing would change?

It was part of our acquisition agreement: it's a Change of Operations clause. There could be no change of operations for three years.

It was in writing.

A Change of Operations clause is key. At some point, some of the people are going to be uncomfortable with the acquisition. And at some point, probably all of them finally will be. There's no perfect way to do it, because you're being acquired most likely by someone who either just wants the bodies—they do what you do, they just want the bodies—or they *don't* do what you do and they don't fully understand and respect it. They say they do, they maybe walk the walk, but in the end they don't. And so at some point something's going to change. So the best thing you can do is protect your people and your business, or the brand you built, for as long as you can. There's probably a Cinderella story where it's perfect and everything works out, but I don't see those in our business, anyway.

I think the Change of Operations clause was the best thing that my leadership did. And we called Capgemini on it many times, where they tried to change something, step over the line with attorneys.

The Change of Operations clause basically said that there were to be no changes in Idean leadership, that all changes within operational procedures had to come from Idean leadership, and that Capgemini couldn't force any changes in our business model and operating procedure. It meant that Capgemini couldn't touch us directly. They could come to our leadership and try to make changes. But if we said no, that was off the table.

Did that Change of Operations clause cover everything?

We still did have to move to their expense reporting systems, which were terrible, and a couple of things like that. But we pushed back on that for probably a year and a half because we tried it and we're like, "It doesn't even work on a Mac. So you want everybody to install Parallels just so we can submit expense reports?" It was time reporting, as well. And it was like, no, we're not doing it. You can get somebody offshore to enter our time for us. We'll send you an export.

They tried to tell us we couldn't have certain tools. Figma was brand new, but Sketch or Photoshop or something? They would say, "No, we don't support that and you can't get a license for it." Okay, I guess we just lock the doors because that's how we do our work. It did get pretty detailed, but the thing was, if you were a studio that was performing well and making money, then they kind of left you alone.

Our business dipped right after acquisition, which is fairly common because you're distracted, you're not paying attention as much. But then it did really pick up. And we still weren't working on any Capgemini projects for a while, so they kind of left us alone for a while.

What happened when that Change of Operations clause stopped being applicable?

They had some influence to get us to work on some stuff, but they didn't have the absolute say. Before that three year mark, we could kind of say no. But we were saying no with less frequency. And then it kind of came to the part where we said, "Okay, it's time to work together now." And that's kind of where the pain started. They're like, "Redesign some SAP screens. We just sold a hundred-million-dollar SAP implementation. Can you design it for us? We need it to be pretty." We got a lot of that "I want it to be pretty" stuff. I would respond, "If research shows it needs to be pretty, it's going to be pretty, but otherwise it's just going to do really what it needs to do."

And honestly, I think one of the important things anybody who's entertaining an acquisition should do with the acquisition partner is really figure out before the acquisition happens, how are you going to work together, and how you fit into their business. And make sure both parties agree. That's what didn't happen with us, and I think that was the only real problem I saw. My leadership disengaged from those conversations, and my peers and I were kind of left holding the bag: we had to try to figure out a way to work together. How do we make this thing fit? And in the end, I don't really think it did fit very well, but we tried to make it as painless as it could be.

Part of it was that they're a consultancy, and being a consultant means every person can kind of do everything. That's what they train consultants to do: to dive in, figure it out, do this job, do that job. They're all just doing a job. It's kind of like a widget. But designers aren't like that. A visual designer can't do interaction design, or vice versa. Some can, yes, but in general they're very siloed practices which augment each other. And they started trying to do our resourcing for us. They would say, "Oh, well, that person's on the bench." But they don't know how to do that. Those were conversations that ate up tons of time and frustrated people. But I think what really started to sour was having to work more and more on their projects which weren't a great fit for a firm like ours.

They were not a fan of us having our own business development team. And when that three year mark hit, they kind of got rid of it. Their people did not know how to sell our stuff, even though we ran workshops and everything on how you sell design services, showing them how it's a consultative sale more so than, "Hey, here's my spec sheet and I got all this stuff. Which ones do you want to buy?" That's kind of how they sell their work. Once we lost our sales team, or most of them anyway, we became more beholden to the work they were selling, which was not fun, sexy, challenging. Actually, it was challenging, but not the type of work we would've ever gone after.

It was like we were an afterthought, and they would start coding an application before we'd even do discovery. And it's like, you're making something nobody's going to use. Then we'd get eight months into a project, or six months into a project, and they'd say, "Well, this kind of sucks."

We would respond, "Yeah, it does suck because you didn't even bother to find out what people need. You listened to a couple engineers and executives say what they need, and that's really not how you make a great product."

It's because they're much more financially motivated than we were. Their main tool is a spreadsheet. And they want to start coding on day one because that means they start burning more revenue on day one. They don't want to backload their revenue. They need to get it this quarter.

How did the designers react to this approach?

We shielded it as much as we could from them. They sensed some things for sure, but we kept a lot of it away from them for the betterment of the work, and for their wellbeing. It wasn't to hide anything, necessarily; I was always much more open about how our business worked with all of my people. I really wanted people to understand it because when I had to ask somebody to do something they didn't want to do, I wanted them to understand why. And it worked very well, and it made a good, close team. But some of these things, the political stuff, the operational stuff, I did try to keep from them. And we did a very good job of fighting that stuff for a long time and winning. That wasn't just me. That was my CEO. That was the rest of our executive team as well.

But in the end, I was there after all of them had left. And so it was kind of me holding the stick. Every one of the C-suite was gone by the time I left. Their earnout stuff had happened, and they had done all the protecting they could. The three-year timeline had run out, so there really wasn't much more for them to do.

It was a pretty large acquisition. Clearly the C-suite benefited financially; did other people see a material reward from the transaction?

Yes. I did; I was a minority equity holder in the business, but they were pretty generous with the equity on who got it. It wasn't enough to retire, but it was a sizable amount of money and it was motivating.

Another great thing my executive team did was that they negotiated additional compensation for certain key people. So for three years, as long as you were employed at the end of each of those years, you got additional compensation. But maybe 70% of the people left that money on the table and left the company. And it was not a small amount of money for some people.

How did the team at Capgemini react to this attrition?

By that point, I'm not even sure how much they cared. Well, I'm sure they cared, but they didn't really do much to stop it, to be honest. Most people got good raises after that, better than we could have given. They did those things to help, but I don't think they knew how to stop it, and it wasn't a big enough problem for them to stop what they were doing to focus on it. We were a blip on the radar for their revenue.

That's what you get when you're in a company of 300,000 people. They run it like a machine, not like this family who cared. Family may be a corny word to use, but at Idean, we were people who cared. Unhappy designers don't do great design work, but that's not really the consulting mindset. The consulting mindset is more like, "Let me crack this whip and you're going to crap out some spreadsheets." And you can't. I can make spreadsheets if I'm in a bad mood, but I couldn't come up with a badass information architecture to handle the super complex problems.

People just saw more and more of their grip coming onto us. And every inch it got closer, something got worse. Whether it's just your time reporting software, then it's this thing or that thing, then it's all the types of projects we're getting. More than anything, it was probably the types of work we were seeing come in. We would say, "Oh, the cool stuff isn't coming in anymore. We're kind of getting stuff that nobody really wants to work on," but we kind of had to suck it up and do it.

For example, we had one very large client from a Capgemini project.

We had an empathy workshop with the client, and it was nothing the client had been through before. Our designers said, "Okay, let's play 'day in the life of your customer', and I want to hear about your customers."

And the client, of all people, described the customer in a *very* derogatory way.

And my team was horrified; "Oh my God, you really don't get what the word empathy means. That's how you think of your customers?"

And it was like that example, over, and over, and over.

They almost always removed our discovery phase. You're just going to throw us into something very complex and very foreign to us? Because I don't know how to create a quoting engine for an insurance company. That's not easy stuff. It's up our alley, but we need to dig in and understand.

And they would say, "No, no, no, don't worry about that. We know what it needs to do. We just need it to look good."

Do you think there are things your team at Idean could have done during the negotiation process to mitigate some of these things?

We needed an integration plan.

We needed to ask, "Do you see us working on projects together? And if so, how?"

We could have laid out general approaches of how the project approach should work. We had the *discover*, *design*, *deliver* approach. We could have asked, "How does this approach look and work in the future? Who contributes what? When do certain resources get pulled onto a project?"

We could have tried to get them excited about that, or at least bought into it. Their opinion might change over time if that's not working, and that makes sense since they're most likely a very financially motivated party. I think you've got to come to that agreement first before you get fully in bed with these people.

But it would've required more change on their part, too. We changed a fair amount to be part of these big, huge implementation deals, and we could have worked on those and been fairly happy, but it needed to accommodate a little more of the design process. And if they would've been willing to shift their pitch process and approach, I think it could have worked.

It seems like finally Accenture might have figured out some of it a little better than they had originally, so maybe they have something that worked. And somehow it worked at McKinsey. So I think it's possible, but it requires pain and effort on both parties.

During all of these fairly negative experiences, did the positive culture you described earlier maintain?

As much as possible. We didn't get to do as much cross-studio stuff, because travel budgets were cut a little. But we had a good relationship within our group and within the people who had been at Idean for a while. We just didn't see each other in person as much anymore.

We did a company trip every year with the whole company prior to being acquired: they went to Hawaii; we took the whole company to Iceland. It cost a lot of money.

But then the last one we had, which was after acquisition, our CEO paid for part of it himself because he was like, "This is happening. This is my last move as CEO. I'm making this happen."

The founders had been at it for 23 or so years. My CEO drove a 1990 Toyota Corolla or something like that when we sold the company. They were not living large. Our company did well, but none of them probably ever made over $200 grand a year before any of this; most of them lived in Palo Alto or New York, where that's not incredible money. I think they deserved to do the sale. And then a lot of other people made a good chunk of money that they wouldn't have gotten anywhere else, and they never counted on. And then they got a better salary for three or so years. At some point you kind of got to let your baby go.

Given what sounds like a not-great experience for you, what would you tell a design leader who is thinking about selling their company?

Make sure you're picking the right partner.

Make sure you all see eye to eye in how you see your business integrating into theirs, or augmenting theirs.

Ask, "What are your goals? Why are you doing this?"

And make sure you cover all of those things, as many of them as you can, in writing.

If you're just looking for a check, who really cares? But if you're looking to keep the thing you've made alive, and keep the people whom you've employed and trained happy and growing, those are bigger concerns. Everybody likes getting a check, and accepting that check and walking away is easy. But the hard parts are protecting your people and protecting the thing you made. And I think that's where most of your work should happen, even more so than the dollar amount that it's for.

Do your due diligence. It's not only the acquirer that needs to do due diligence. You need to really figure out what you want to get out of it, and put in safeguards to make sure you get those things. And I think those things are: no change of operations, retention bonuses for key employees, and making sure some of your employees have stock in the company before the sale—because as many people as possible should benefit from these things.

Getting It in Writing

Matthew described that his management team wrote specific guidelines into the sale agreement related to changes in operating process and structure. Gavin explained that he "should have given everyone a raise before closing the deal, because now all of a sudden, you're dealing with HR and policies that have been around for a decade." Terms related to operations would have helped both of them, but aren't things that are typically in a contract "by default."

In addition to the basics (the money! and the "lawyer stuff" like indemnification and representations), these are the things that *are* typically covered in a sale agreement:

- *What is actually being purchased.* In an asset sale, you are probably selling everything, but what constitutes everything? The assets, including liabilities, contracts, intellectual property, and so-on will be spelled out. Additionally, things that *aren't* being purchased will be listed, too, as excluded assets.

- *Terms about competition and solicitation.* If you leave, are you able to work with your clients again? What about your employees—can you bring them with you to start a new company? Chances are, you'll be tied to a material non-compete and non-solicit (perhaps as long as five years). Play this one out in your head: if the deal goes south and you leave early, as did Maria at Facebook, can you actually do what you love?

- *What you can and can't talk about.* Your contract will add details about confidentiality which will likely extend a standard NDA by *a lot*. What happens when you want to write a book (like this!) in the future—will you be able to share your experiences with the world?

Of course, you can also negotiate for any terms you like, and if both parties are willing to accept them, they'll become binding—and *theoretically*—will be followed after the transaction closes. I'll come back to *theoretically* in a moment.

These are some of the things that you might want to negotiate and get in writing:

- *I want the ability to sign off on my contracts.* In a larger organization, you'll likely assume their legal process, which may extend a negotiation by a large amount of time. If it's important to you to close business quickly, control over the legal process (even using your own outside counsel instead of the corporate team) may be to your advantage.

- *I want to be clear on how I "get credit" for selling work.* If you have an earnout, it will probably be tied to revenue. But if a sale includes people from outside your organization, how do you claim that you were responsible for the revenue? Phil described that, at Deloitte, there was a very complicated formula for this; is that formula in writing, and do you understand it?

- *I want to retain control of my brand.* Is it important to you that your brand aesthetic and message continue on? More on this later.

- *I want the ability to spend my budget as I see fit.* Gavin mentioned discretionary spending; will you be able to send your whole team on a vacation, if you feel that they've earned it, without getting approval?

- *I want the ability to hire, fire, and give raises without approval.* Often, acquiring companies will centralize HR functions, and so you may lose control over your resourcing. Are you ready to work on a hiring schedule, and in a hiring process, which you don't oversee? What about spot bonuses or raises—has that been a fundamental part of your culture?

- *I want to keep my rate structure.* The acquiring company may not agree with your bill rates, or may want to standardize. Will this disrupt the way you interact with current clients, or change your ability to attract new ones?

- *I want the same terms (or better ones) if the buyer later sells their company.* If you have unvested stock, does it accelerate? Do the things you've negotiated for transfer to the new owners, or do you have to substantiate your requests all over again?

- *I want money to spend to help retain my team after the acquisition.* This is sometimes called a management carveout: an amount of money is set aside from the deal that can be used to provide retention incentive to your key team members. But that money is coming from somewhere; are you okay with it coming out of your share of the sale?

- *I want my money if I get fired.* It doesn't make a lot of sense for a buyer to acquire your company and then fire people, but lots of things in business don't make sense. Have you played out the various scenarios that might lead to a termination?

The main reason to argue for these things is that, if push comes to shove, you'll be on firm legal grounds to come back to where you started. When I first started being involved in working with contracts at frog, David Kramer, the GM, gave me some great advice. He said, "Pretend that the person you signed with isn't there any more, and has been replaced by someone terrible." We assume best intentions from the people we've established relationships with, and it can be easy to give them the benefit of the doubt: "Oh, we talked about that, I'm sure they'll remember if it ever came to it." But people change jobs, and their replacement won't know about those casual conversations—and they probably won't care about them, either.

Of course, you can always push too hard. When you demand things to be included in the contract, it starts to send a signal to the buyer—that you don't trust them. And just because you ask for these things doesn't mean you'll get them. *And*, each item you want to put in the contract requires conversation, negotiation, and time (and, of course, lawyer fees at upwards of $600 an hour).

And back to the comment about things being binding, but only *theoretically*. Imagine that you've gotten to a place after the transaction that is so bad and so painful that you consider going back to the contract for "proof." If you push back, legally, you'll make the emotional environment worse. You'll be back to the same feelings of anxiety that you likely had during the original sale. You'll probably return to the secrecy part, so you don't further disrupt your team; or, you'll be out in the open about it, and your team morale will dip even lower. And, it's likely that the buyer has bigger and better lawyers than you do. It's incidental for them to drag out a legal process; it's probably not for you.

So it's in your best interest to assume the contract is a collaboratively-agreed set of terms, and in a worst case scenario, you could lean on it—but you probably won't.

Crystal Rutland, Who Founded Particle Design and Sold It to Wind River in 2021

After working inhouse at Intel, Crystal founded Empirical, and then Particle Design. The focus of the company was on meaningful innovation in emerging technology; the team worked with Samsung, Dreamworks and Hyperloop One. She sold Particle to Wind River after five years.

Tell me a little about the company you built.

I ran a UX-design agency. Our customers called us a mini IDEO. We did a lot of futures work; I came out of Intel and started my agency after I left Intel, and they were our first big customer. We worked with companies like Jaguar, Land Rover, and Samsung, doing concept-design work. For example, we would ask, "What is AI and computing going to look like for Intel's chipset roadmap?" Or, "What would cars look like five years from now? What current technology that exists today, like AR, or AI, is going to influence how they are going to design their cars in the future?" We looked at the infotainment systems, and how the communication happens between the driver and the car.

When I sold the company, we were a small team. We've flexed up and down over the years, and at one point we were up to 32 or 33 people, maybe closer to 40, with regular contractors and stuff. But at the time of selling, we were like nine or ten people.

When we were small initially, even our clients who loved us were hesitant to give us large projects, because it would represent too much of our revenues. Once we were able to get bigger in size, we were able to take on more interesting large-scale projects. And then once I scaled back down, we already had a reputation for doing those larger programs. We basically became this boutique agency that was doing these huge projects, even though we weren't very big. And that's the stage we were in when we got acquired.

What was the culture of the company like before you sold it?

Our culture was very loose, very self-organized, self-driven. We never had account managers, or project managers, or anything like that. Everybody was a UX designer or a researcher, every single person except for the office manager or the finance person. Every person who was there was actually doing UX work. So each team member had to be very self-organized and self-driven. There were different levels of experience, but no hierarchy: it was completely flat. It was extremely collaborative.

I had an employee, and she wasn't a great fit for the company. She was really bright and I really liked her a lot, but when we sat down for a one-on-one one day after I'd been running the company for five or six years, she said, "I just don't understand who's in charge. It's very inefficient." She was very frustrated with the way the process worked. And I was frozen, and thought, "Oh my God, who *is* in charge? I'm so irresponsible. How can I be running a company and not have an answer for her?"

I slept on it, and walked and thought for a couple days, and in our next one-on-one, I was like, "Okay, here's the deal. This was a great question you asked me, and I'm going to tell you. *The idea is in charge.* Everything that you're describing in the process might feel inefficient, but in the long run, it's literally the most efficient way to move forward with the right designs."

She left the company. But it was a really, really good crisis moment. The process can feel chaotic and it can *feel* inefficient, but it drives clarity rather than chaos. This wasn't a culture for everybody, but it was a really important reflection of how culture starts with leadership. It was a very important reflection of how I work and live in the world and approach creativity. So we always hope to build an environment where *the idea could be in charge*, and the idea could take the lead and help us understand where we should go.

Why did you start to think about selling?

I was so exhausted. I was just done. I actually had been done for a while. I said to myself, "Okay, I've got this five-year plan. I don't *want* to do this for five more years, but I could do it in order to get an exit." So I knew that I was working towards an exit.

I just loved it, and there are so many things that I love about running a company. But I was just really tired. I had raised my son as a single mom, and when he was in high school, I started the agency thinking that by the time he graduated and was done with college, I would exit.

It's a lot of work building a company, so you want to get something out of it. You hope that it leads to being able to do something else interesting afterwards. I didn't want to think, "I put all that effort in it, and for what? I'm just going to walk away and build something else again?" Building something is fucking hard. It's really hard. When we were up to 30 to 40 people, it was awesome because it just became like an engine that was sustaining itself. But the numbers were also so big at that time that it became scary.

What was the hardest part?

Business development. It was very exhausting being responsible for all of those salaries. There was a point at which, when we were up to a really big company, our overhead was like $350k to $400K a month. It was so expensive that, if some transitions happened with our customers and there would be a falloff, it would be like, "Well, shit." When your overhead is that much, you can flip underwater really fast. It's what made me want to scale back.

I always felt like I was on a razor's edge. With four-to-six months of bad management, I could go underwater. I could flip this thing underwater in a way that I could never recover in my personal life. I could never make that kind of money to get out of the kind of debt that it would be. I was personally guaranteeing almost everything, because the bank wasn't going to give me anything. So I was personally guaranteeing my property against the business.

I've worked my whole life; I'm a single mom, and I was very poor growing up. It was a Herculean effort for me to get from where I started to where I am now. And the idea that I would've asked my family to sacrifice for all those years, and then I would be not only bankrupt, but in a hole that took me years to get out of; that was unacceptable to me.

It just became really scary. If at some point I could've transitioned to where the business wasn't tied to my personal finances, then maybe it would've been fine.

I always wanted to have cash flow four months out. I had a line of credit; I would have a three-month runway with no debt, and then a couple months after that with debt. But I was never, ever more than six months away from just total collapse, ever. Even at the $400K-a-month point.

Because even though I had big clients, it was like they were still on quarterly and annual-budget cycles. Nobody was signing me a two-year contract. I would have a client for two, three years constantly, and most of my clients just kept going. I had very little client turnover for the most part. But still, you don't know. If all of a sudden they get hit with a budget crunch... I had a lot of contracts that were mostly renewed quarterly, but they could also just get dropped.

Tell me about what happened when you decided to sell the business.

I said, "Okay, I'm getting ready to sell this, I think." I had a list, with first tier and second tier companies that could acquire us. I had three customers that I was working for regularly, and I had an interest in having them acquire us; that was my first-tier list. These were customers that I trusted and that I could say to, "Hey, I have something to tell you... here's what I'm thinking of doing." They were three people who I wanted to tell anyway, because we were doing really important work for them, and if they wanted to have us finish some things out, I wanted them to also just have the heads-up.

There was interest, and it became very clear that one particular customer became an early front-runner. Wind River, who acquired us, pulled out ahead.

How did they start to pull ahead?

Through the conversations, it became clear that we would be able to all go as a team. They were going to want us to retain some of our culture. I have a one-pager on our culture, and I supplied it to my executive sponsors at Wind River. The people who were in charge of their acquisition process were excited about that culture sheet, and told me, "We like this. We don't want to hurt your culture when you come in." Everyone says that, and I know there are mixed results, but the results have been pretty good.

When it became clear that you were going to pursue something with Wind River, what happened next?

We had two sponsors inside of the organization. They pitched it internally to their corporate development team; the Head of Corporate Development reached out, and that's when the brass tacks started. Within three months of the initial conversation where I told my clients, "I'm looking to be acquired," I was in conversations on brass tacks, maybe even sooner. Because they wanted to move really quickly. In the original conversation, they wanted to close within 90 days. It actually ended up taking eight and a half months. We really thought it was going to close sooner, because it was all agreed upon. But the back-and-forths, it just takes a long time.

How did you get to a number that you agreed upon so quickly?

I'm pretty sure I let them make an offer that I then replied to. I had a number in mind. And the way I arrived at the number that was going to be acceptable to me was basically one-and-a-half to two times EBITDA. EBITDA is pretty close to gross in my business because there's not a lot of overhead. Most of my costs are labor, which is not accounted for in EBITDA. So basically it was one-and-a-half to two times gross revenue.

I arrived at that number by looking around online. I'm a service organization, not a product organization. My value is my people and their expertise, and you don't really get a big return for that. Luckily for us, right before we started talking brass tacks, we happened to sign just a huge contract, the largest contract I'd ever signed by far with a customer. And it was a full year, not quarter by quarter.

Because it was longer term, it was a big-size contract and it had some degree of built-in stability. That looked really attractive to the buyer, because it signaled that "these people can pay for themselves, too, if they finish out this contract."

In addition to the money in the transaction, we also discussed stock in their company. They were run by an investment company, and their company was likely going to sell to somebody else in a short time, within a few years after we were acquired. That was their stated goal: to find someone to acquire Wind River. And so the stock became important to think about because it might be worth something. I didn't focus on that, because the stock would only be of value if they found a buyer, and who knows what price they'd find that at, right?

I was very lucky that Wind River actually *did* get acquired within a year of them acquiring us. So not only did all that stock actually end up paying out, but then there were new deals that were part of the acquisition that came to me and some members of my team.

In addition to the money and stock, what was really important to me was that the team was going to stay together, and that we were going to have a place inside this company. They were going to retain our brand, our website, our name, everything was going to be retained. And they did it. They still actually refer to us as Particle Design, even though we're part of their company.

The culture part wasn't in any of the paperwork. They said, "Well, we can run our company however we want. We're not going to pre-commit to you. Once you get in here, we might decide we don't want you all to be together. We can't promise you that you'll stay together. But we're saying that is our intention." It was one of the first parts of the conversations that I was having.

Before we selected Wind River, one of the potential buyers we were talking to almost certainly wasn't going to bring us all in as a whole team. That immediately put them in last place. The team part was really important.

The other thing that was important to me was that the purchase price was not contingent on me staying with the company. They could give me extra bonuses and stuff to try to retain me, that was cool. But my price was my price. And if I got in there, and I hated it, and I wanted to leave, I was still going to get paid. That was also a really important negotiating point, and they were fine with that. They just put a clause in there that if I left without due cause, they could delay paying me for three years.

There was some penalty. They wanted some reason for me to stay. And I was like, "Okay, that's fine."

I also had to sign a pretty steep non-compete that I wouldn't go to another agency, and that I wouldn't go work for one of their competitors as a lead UX for five years. My lawyer told me, "That's a pretty severe non-compete. I would go for three years, not five. I wouldn't sign a five-year non-compete if I were you." But I just went ahead and did it. I don't know if I regret that or not. Five years is a long time. I would actually probably recommend that people take my lawyer's advice and sign a shorter non-compete.

What other regrets do you have about the compensation package, or things you wished you had done differently?

I regretted the purchase price pretty quickly.

I thought, "Man, I really didn't ask for enough." I was a little too afraid of the deal not going through, because I was so tired. I was a little bit too fear-based. I was just exhausted.

All of this happened during COVID, and I was actually in Vietnam working on lockdown with a client that we had there. It was just a really very exhausting time. Just when the country was opening up here in the US, I went to Vietnam and they were just shutting down, because we were on different schedules of fighting COVID.

So imagine: I was trying to finalize the deal and I was trying to keep up on all the work, and on the heels of being in lockdown for 18 months, I went to a foreign country to be in lockdown there, and it was a much more severe lockdown.

It was just a lot. I was working from a little bit more of a fear-based place than I like to operate from. So I regretted that I didn't push back harder on the price. Luckily for me, the company then got acquired, and all of the perks associated with that acquisition got me to where I wished I had been on the price, and now I'm just in a pretty good spot. But that's a real luck thing. It's a very unusual situation where you get acquired, and then who acquired you gets acquired. That's very unusual.

How much more do you think you could have negotiated for up front?

Probably like 20–40% more. What we do is so unique, and it's very difficult to express value when you're a service company and it's really based on your talent. But I think they would've gone with 25% more, without a doubt.

But I was just tired. I said, "I really want this deal to go through and I want to move into a new phase."

I remember talking to someone who sold his company many years before I did. He told me, "Crystal, it's not about your purchase price. It's about your compensation, and your bonuses, and everything that the company wants after you get acquired. Almost everyone is disappointed with their purchase price. Because it just really isn't that much at the end of the day. Once everything is factored in, once taxes and everything else is factored in, most people feel pretty flat. So make sure you're negotiating your position, and your salary, and your benefits in the new company really well, because that is a part of your purchase price. You should just think of that as part of your purchase price."

He had given me that advice many years before, and I was so far away from selling the company at that point that I was like, "Okay, whatever. That's a privileged position." But I found it in retrospect to be very true. And I was keeping it in mind when I was negotiating what my position would be in the new company.

Were the things like your new compensation and your title in writing in the contract you signed?

No, but it was in an attachment; it was like a Human Resources document. I don't think it was even an addendum in the contract. I think it was just in a different document that was not signed, but that we agreed to. It was emailed to me that this was going to be the situation, and I remember being surprised by that. Titles and salaries—I don't even think they were referenced. I just trusted them.

You mentioned the deal took a lot longer than the 90 days they originally intended. Once you had the negotiation part finished, what took the most time to get the deal done?

We very quickly agreed on the price. We pretty quickly agreed on the other things. And it still just took forever. The negotiation was at least 100 or 150 hours, and maybe 35 or 40 conversations. It was a lot. And then they sent me a list that had all the documents they needed. My VP of Finance and Operations was the one who pulled it all together, and she probably spent a couple hundred hours on that, and then I probably spent a hundred hours. It was a lot of hours. It was so much time.

So they had this very huge Excel spreadsheet for corporate acquisition, for acquisitions. It was like 180 or 250 rows in this Excel document of things for us to fill out. A lot of them didn't apply to us, they applied to other kinds of companies. But probably 60 or 70 of them were filled with things we needed to get to them. It was insane.

And then that looped back-and-forth a couple times, and we had to revise it. I kept asking "What is taking so long?" It would get to us, and our lawyers needed a week to review it and to get them a response, and then their lawyers needed a week or two to review it and to get us a response. And then pretty soon it's like five months later.

I was doing this from a hotel room in Vietnam. There was just a lot of fear of like, "Maybe this isn't going to go through. It's taking so long."

Another thing that stretched out the timeline was that their board had to review everything. Originally, they didn't approve the salaries that we requested for the team, because the new salaries represented too much of an uptick from what they were earning at Particle.

Particle was a really unique agency. We were doing really cool work, and all of our people were super senior. Almost all of the team took a significant pay cut to work for us, because the work we did was so cool and so interesting. There's a reason our clients called us a mini IDEO; there are so few places to do the kind of work we were doing. We were competing against frog and other very large, very reputable agencies, and winning. We were doing cool shit, working with companies like Hyperloop to explore the future of transportation.

HR did get their salaries up to the very max of what the board would approve, but it was really hard for the board to understand that people would work for less at our company, and I had to argue why these salary upticks were important.

Are you glad you sold Particle?

My acquisition is a best-case scenario in many ways. Everybody at Wind River seemed very transparent. We felt like, "These are our people; they have a similar culture. Even though they're really big, they have more of a startup culture. They seem to welcome people to talk."

During the negotiations, my business partner and I were having a lot of conversations like, "What do we think it would be like to be in this culture?" We did a lot of due diligence before we even approached anyone for buying us, thinking, "What is that culture going to be like there?" We took our best guess at what the culture would be. We said, "We're not going to sell to anyone— unless we get desperate—who doesn't have a culture that seems similar enough."

I was very clear on what I wanted out of the sale. It took some work to get to that clarity: a lot of walking, and meditating, and writing, and talking with my partner. It was very nice to have somebody else who I trusted involved.

And when we got into Wind River, it turned out that we were 100% correct. Our sponsors vowed to us that they would protect us once we got in, and I had a high-trust relationship with those sponsors. I had a meeting with their CEO well before I agreed to be acquired. We had a really, really great conversation. And after that conversation, which also took place in Vietnam in a hotel room over Zoom, I thought, "Yes, this is going to be good." And it was, and it still is.

Do you have any advice for people considering selling their companies?

Yes; here are my "top 6 advice hits":

1. Get as clear as possible about what you want before you start the process of selling your company. What is most important to you? What will you not compromise on? What does your post-acquisition day to day look like?

2. Make sure you have a great lawyer and financial advisor. Even though I had a lawyer and finance person, they were not the best and so I missed out on some important advice and was mostly alone in navigating the process.

3. It isn't just about the purchase price. Make sure you negotiate a good landing position and salary / bonus / stock package for yourself and your management team.

4. If your culture is important to you, make sure you discuss it early and often. I sent our buyer an excerpt from our Employee Handbook which helped them understand our culture. I used it actively and intentionally to serve as a conversation starter and indicator of what it would be like to work with the senior management inside the acquiring company.

5. If your team is important to you, protect them. Keep them at the center of conversations with the acquiring company. If you cannot agree on everything you want pre-acquisition (I could not), make sure you have frank conversations about what you will expect from HR post-acquisition.

6. Get the highest title you can in the acquiring company. This will ensure you have the most control over your destiny post-purchase.

Diligence

Crystal described a seemingly never-ending back-and-forth with lawyers, focused on collecting various documents. This diligence phase is one of the most time-consuming and trying parts of the process; many designers seem to have an allergic reaction to spreadsheets, and this part of the process is all about contracts, estimates, forecasts, and the nuts and bolts of the business.

Before you go through a process like this, it's hard to really internalize just how thorough, and time consuming, this part can be. I was warned it was all encompassing; it was, to the point of straining my marriage and personal relationships.

If you were methodical in how you ran the operations of your company, you'll have nicely organized folders with MSAs, SOWs, and change orders. You'll have your invoices sorted, your accounts payable detailed, and you'll be able to find any part of your business at the drop of the hat. But for most of us, we weren't that thoughtful and organized (particularly when we started). That employee you terminated years ago—can you find her I9? What about the lease agreement for your building? And that client that you invoiced by hand before you used Quickbooks, years ago; who was that again, and how much was it for?

It seems crazy, but that's the level of detail you'll need to provide during diligence. The hardest part of this process will be finding documentation related to anomalies, like contracts that ended prematurely or change orders that impacted revenue. But the sheer tedium of aggregating the documents that are produced in the normal course of business can feel overwhelming.

Here are some of the things that you'll be expected to present during this due diligence process in a spreadsheet similar to the one Crystal described:

Contracts

The most time consuming part of preparing for diligence is aggregating your contracts. There are different types of acquisitions, but in an asset purchase, contracts are assigned to the buyer, so they'll want to know what they are signing up for. This is every MSA, every SOW, every change order, every NDA—anything that a buyer may inherit as a liability, or that may be in conflict with their existing contracts. Some of the things they'll look for include:

- Clauses related to *assignment*. Generally, contracts can be assigned to another party, unless there are terms that explicitly prohibit or limit this. When you assign the contract to the buyer, they take on all of the terms. If the contract limits assignment, you might see language like this:

  > *This Agreement shall be binding upon and inure to the benefit of each Party and each of its applicable successors and assigns. This Agreement and the rights hereunder are personal to the Contractor and shall not be transferred, assigned, sub-contracted or sublicensed in any manner, pledged or otherwise encumbered by the Contractor, whether voluntarily, involuntarily, by operation of law or otherwise without Company's prior written consent. Company may without restriction assign this Agreement and its rights and obligations hereunder.*

  Your sale terms may require you to go hunt down that assignment approval in writing, and that means you'll have to let your clients know a deal is pending.

  I found that, early in the history of my company, I ignored Assignment terms entirely in my contracts because it never occurred to me that I might want to turn the contract over to someone else. It's worth creating a short spreadsheet that tracks requirements related to assignment.

- Clauses related to *non-competes*. Some contracts limit the companies you can work with, either by industry or by name. This may pose a problem for a buyer, particularly if they already have a contract with one of those named companies.

- Descriptions of how you invoice and bill. I've found that companies that are used to billing based on time and materials (strictly hourly) have a hard time understanding the mechanics of deliverable-based invoicing and its relationship to revenue recognition. Prepare yourself to explain, over and over and over, the nuances of how you know when a design is "done" and what "acceptance" means in our industry.

In diligence, a buyer will also look at your invoices, and will likely compare some of your historic invoices to the terms of your contracts. They are looking to see if you are buttoned-up in your operations, but also to understand if they are opening themselves to risk based on how closely you adhere to your contractual commitments.

Buyers will also look at your lease agreements, again for terms related to assignment, and also for commitments to duration and rent increases.

Finances

I found that preparing finances for diligence was actually one of the easiest parts of this process for me, and for many of the people I spoke with who managed small or mid-sized agencies, because design businesses are often pretty simple in structure. Our companies probably have cash on hand, some forms of credit and debt (typically carried on a credit card), and some basic equity structure. Beyond that, designers typically don't poke around in more complex financial vehicles or investments.

One of the parts of the financial review process that has some unique aspects in the context of a design business relates to hourly rates and utilization rates. In a simple T&E model, an employee gets paid a certain amount and works a certain amount of hours. It's easy to calculate their hourly rate, and it's easy to calculate how much they are working and if they are *fully utilized*—working a full 40 hours a week.

Smaller consultancies break this model. Designers often work on many projects at once, or casually help out with a program through collaborative sketching and brainstorming. They may not track time diligently, and may not even track it at all. Designers "just want to do the work" and so it becomes very difficult to claim a studio-wide utilization rate with a strong degree of confidence. But a buyer wants to know how hard people are working, and without a utilization rate, it's hard to know how optimized your studio is. *Optimized* isn't typically something we think about, but it's something a buyer will think about.

But a part of the process that is truly confounding is the Quality of Earnings evaluation. I'm not sure every company goes through this process, but it's a very foreign way of thinking for many designers. The QofE report looks at, among other things, how you recognize the revenue you take in. You run your company on a cash or accrual basis, but there's more to it than that. Consider if you can answer these questions:

- Do you feel that you've earned your revenue when you finish a whole project, or a deliverable? What constitutes "finishing" a deliverable?

- Do you invoice for a percentage of the project before you start, as a form of good-will on signature? When can you claim that you've earned that money?

- Do you have sufficient money in the bank to pay back all of those upon-signature payments if the clients back out?

These aren't things I ever cared about when I ran my company, but an acquirer will care about them a lot. I'm not sure there's anything to do to prepare for a Quality of Earnings investigation ahead of time, except to have given these topics some thought so you have a thoughtful answer (even if the answer is, "I have no idea").

Employees

The diligence process will get into the details of your employees. At the minimum, a buyer will want to understand how many people you employ, if they are full or part time, how long they've been at the company, and how much you pay them. They'll also probably want to understand titles and the way titles relate to experience, if there's a reporting structure, and how many of your employees are utilized at any given time (people who are actually doing the work).

You'll be asked to provide a list of key players, and to describe who would be most likely to take over for you and your leadership team over time. And you'll likely be asked to provide employee records for the last three years, including start date, end date, salaries, titles, and any anomalous behavior (like a performance plan).

Customers

At some point, your buyer will want to talk with your clients. This is a reference check, and once your client knows about your sale, the "cat is out of the bag." Secrets don't stay secret very long, and designers gossip. I would assume that once you get to a customer reference check, the circle of people who know about your sale will widen; this means that, around this time, you'll need to have a solid talk track in place to explain the sale to your employees and clients (even those who aren't interviewed as part of the diligence process).

There's a risk of the customer reference check; your customers may become scared. Will they continue to get the hands-on support they've grown accustomed to? Will their main contacts at your company change? What about pricing? Phil described that after Deloitte bought his company, "The rate increase was astronomical... a doubling or a tripling of our rates."

There's also a risk, although hopefully a small one, that your customer won't say supportive things about you and your business. I always pre-game my conversation with that contact and ask them what they'll talk about, and I trust that they'll be honest, but you never know, and not knowing is risky.

Getting ahead of diligence

Even if you aren't actually interested in selling your company, this might be a good time to do some reflecting on your organizational process. If your feet were held to the fire right now, could you go track down a specific invoice for a specific client? Could you identify how much money you made 14, 20, or 26 months ago? Could you see if, upon acquisition, you are legally allowed to assign an MSA you have with your biggest client? This is a good thought exercise to try prior to beginning an acquisition process, so you can really get a feel for what you might be diving into.

A quick checklist of improvements you might make to get ready for a process like this includes:

- Contract organization. Put all executed contracts in one place, with each client in a unique folder. Create a spreadsheet going back at least 3 years that lists each one, executed dates, and pricing. Identify which have clauses about assignability, and document those contracts in the spreadsheet.

- Employee history. Create a list of active and previous employees, including their start date, end date, salary, and title. Identify any performance issues.

- Revenue history. Produce a detailed historic view of revenue by client by month, revenue by project per month, and revenue attributed to a specific employee. Write a brief description of how you recognize revenue and how you bill.

- Employee utilization. Create a historic view of how many hours each team member worked, their bill rate, and the overall company utilization rates.

You can find a more comprehensive list of documents in the Appendix.

Chris Conley, Who Founded gravitytank and Then Sold It to Salesforce in 2016

Next, let's hear from Chris, who started gravitytank in 1999. His company focused on innovation well before it was common language in design and business, and established a strong reputation for mature, thoughtful and respected design. gravitytank sold in 2016 to Salesforce; Chris left the company upon acquisition.

In the almost 20 years of running gravitytank, did you ever entertain a sale prior to your exit to Salesforce?

Yes. Our first go-around with an acquisition was with an advertising firm that we had worked with. They approached us to see if we were interested. Advertising wouldn't be our first selection, but we had done some projects with them and their clients. We thought we could add a lot of value by combining the problem solving that an innovation firm does with the campaign creation of the advertising firm—the power was in doing those things together.

We had experienced this way of working in the past. When we worked with OfficeMax, their Head of Marketing was very integrated with our work. Our product development and design teams seamlessly worked with their marketing and advertising teams. We built a multibillion-dollar private label together.

We saw this potential acquisition from the advertising company as a possibility of doing that same type of work with different brands, where we could create new products and services and integrate that with marketing.

But the thing that blew the deal was compensation for the staff.

At gravitytank, we made sure that everybody had good, but not extraordinary, salaries. They were above-average for the industry, but not egregious. And then, in every year that was working very well, we had a pot of money left at the end that we could split up between investments, staff bonuses, special activities, and the partners. That's how we ran it for our whole existence. And it worked very well because during the year, we didn't put the firm at risk. We saw other companies that paid more money, but any time they had lumpy revenue, they would start to make bad decisions about projects to take or things to do at the end of the year to try to make the revenue happen. So we said, "We'll feast at the end." We just held off for a reward at the end.

Toward the end of the negotiations, the advertising firm said, "Here's how we're going to handle compensation." We said, "Well, we'd like to handle it this other way, because that's how we've been doing it for the whole duration of the company. If we're responsible for our own P&L, we're not going to move to your compensation structure."

They responded, "Oh, well, let's see... We'll figure it out. We'll figure it out."

Meanwhile, the deadline was getting closer, and it wasn't getting figured out. So we finally called them on it and said, "Hey, let's work this out."

They responded, "Well, it's not going to happen. Global headquarters says they can't do it." And so we said, "Okay, it's not going to work then." We made a pretty fast decision that it just didn't feel right. We thought, "If we can't work this out when we have leverage, then never mind." And that was the end of that.

Several years later, we were acquired by Salesforce.

We had done some work with Salesforce in the past. They were interested and convinced they wanted to acquire us, and it was a fairly easy process to work through because we were a strategic acquisition for them, not revenue accretive. They weren't interested in buying us to increase their EPS. They were acquiring us to more than double the size of their internal design and strategy group and give themselves far more capacity. It was an acquisition of a methodology and approach, and of people.

Your first go-around didn't feel right, but the Salesforce acquisition did. How did you know it would be a good fit?

For owners who are thinking about being acquired, it's important to do diligence about your *own* firm, where the value is, what you have figured out and how you think you should be valued. And equally as important is working with the other firm and collaborating a little bit on how it will work with the other management team—doing some projects together before the acquisition.

Because during the negotiations, you're still dancing. Once you're acquired, you become employees of the other firm, and all your negotiating power is gone. Especially if it's a big company; things change.

So we treated the acquisition process like one of our regular projects. We tried to put everything through a reflective research, collaboration, synthesis lens to try to frame up what it would be and what it would look like. How is this going to work? Where will we be in the organization?

We tried to grab enough time with the other management team to really meet with each other: to run through some scenarios, reflect back on the projects we had done together, and identify what they were hoping for in the type of work we were going to do together. These meetings were pretty tangible—getting stuff up on the walls, focusing on the categories of things we need to talk about; diagramming some things, visualizing structures, flows, workflows; showing how we can talk about the market and types of projects we could run.

As somebody who's a target of an acquisition, deploying your actual skills and mindsets and ways of working is a two-part advantage. First, you're working the problem like you know how to work problems, which is great. You don't feel like you're playing the lawyer's or investment banker's game, or the M&A game. You're saying, "No, here's how we're going to do it." Or, "Here's what we'd like to do because we think it's important to the success of the integration."

Second, you're giving the potential acquirer an authentic exposure to how you'll be working together and how you think about things. If you're working authentically, you're not constantly questioning, and so you start to say authentic things out loud. You say these things early—things like, "Well, we wouldn't be doing this like this if the acquisition happens..."—and if they're like, "Oh, nevermind," you want it to end as fast as possible if it's not going to work out.

Those meetings were the business side of it, the practice side of it, and of course, we were exploring how we liked each other. We had a unique culture in that we all liked each other, for the most part. Going cold turkey into a non-warm culture would be really troublesome. We saw a positive culture in Salesforce. Marc Benioff was very social-impact-forward. He focused on the softer side of things for employees, like maternity leave, social impact work, paid volunteer days. Those were the cultural things that came out during these meetings that reinforced that, "Maybe this is a really good acquisition."

How long did you spend exploring ways of working to see if there was a good match?

We spent about 80 hours in those meetings, but you can ask for only so much of their time. You get into the negotiations and once they have committed to it, they're like, "Come on. This is great. Let's get it done." And then you're worrying, "Are we screwing this up? What are they thinking? How serious are they about this?" So you're doing all those things just as you would in, I don't know, selling your house or a real estate transaction. It's the same things that are going on in your head.

I don't like a lot of legalese about "if this, then that." I prefer it to be very clean. And I believe that a good acquisition, one that's not nitpicking, has enough room on both sides that you're feeling good about it. You say to yourself and your team, "Okay, all in all, we figured this out and we'll accept the consequences. We can't predict the future, but we've worked in a way that we feel good about and we understand enough." If you're trying to minimize all your risk and let them take on all the risk, you have to understand that it's a risk for both parties in the transaction. You have to be clear as an owner of why you're doing it, and then inform yourself about M&A practices.

I drew on this firm called Equiteq who publishes annual reports of mergers and acquisitions for consulting-type firms. They discuss the going multiples of EBITDA and revenue, and financial things like that. Our overall package was two to three times revenue, probably. It's not rocket science. But as a consulting firm or as a design firm or an innovation firm, I think you have to get knowledgeable about this type of information.

Valuation depends on what your revenues are and what your ownership structure is. We had a very wide ownership. We had over eight partners with equity; it's rare for a firm our size to have such a flat or such a spread leadership structure, which I think is why we got the multiple we did—there were so many consulting leaders in the firm, and it wasn't like this pyramid where one person's going to make out really big and everybody else is going to get maybe a nice bump in salary and some restricted stock units. It's actually quite broad with the number of people who were a significant part of the acquisition.

Three of the partners were already pulling back from the day-to-day—myself, my spouse, who was a partner in the firm, and our other partner Michael Winnick, who was running our spin out, dscout. The new generation of leadership was running the firm for the most part. There was an assumption that the three of us wouldn't go along with the acquisition. If they would've put that as a negotiating thing, I would've been like, "Sure, no problem. You want me for a year or two or whatever, sure." But I didn't have to. And I guess as an entrepreneur, one of the things I value most is flexibility. And so if they weren't going to require it, I wasn't going to necessarily go along.

Before the acquisition, we had started to develop the next generation of leadership and management in our company. The COO and I were starting to pull back and just play a role on the broad strategic parts of the business. We were building the management structure for the next generation to grow. This next group of leaders were great at their craft, and good at growing accounts if they already existed, but they didn't want to have to go get new business. We had discussions about partnering, and they said, "We'd rather work on the work and not have to worry about the business development." That made it clear that we would be open to the right acquisition.

During the negotiations, my younger partners weren't asking for us to stick around post-sale. They said, "We got this," and, "We're excited about this."

It sounds like the partners were excited about the transaction, and the next level of leadership was, too. What did the rest of the employees think when the acquisition was announced?

During the process, probably 10% of the company knew about it—8 to 10 people. People knew that we were speaking with companies, that we were getting interest; we were upfront about that. And we described that we would have to keep it confidential even amongst us. But at some point, when it looked like it was going to happen, we had a meeting with the team. And at that point, even, because I think maybe people knew about the advertising firm that fell through, some people were like, "I don't believe it's going to happen."

But it's a little hard to know how the team felt after the acquisition. I wouldn't use the term happy, because there's so much uncertainty about the future at that point. I think designers and innovators can be just as risk averse as anybody else. So in their minds it's like, "Well, what's it really going to be like?" I think it's probably a bell curve: there were some people who didn't go along and they left, beforehand. And then you have the big middle who are like, "Yeah, let's see what happens." Everybody got a raise. Everybody got some stock and everybody got more benefits. So the professional compensation part was great, very fair.

And then there's probably some people who are very excited for the opportunities that were going to open up. Basically, we went from "hoping" to work with the CEOs of companies, to walking in the front door in the biggest, most interesting companies in the world and doing work for them. A lot of people got amazing experiences very quickly with great audiences, strategic design, and digital transformation. A year in, some people found another group in Salesforce and moved overseas.

Like I mentioned, I wasn't intimately involved in all the workshop meetings with Salesforce and stuff like that, when they were figuring out how it would work. When we talked about it with the whole staff, I gave it my blessing and said, "I'm really cool with it." But I didn't help people process it in an authentic way as I should have done. I was trying to be careful not stepping on the other leaders' toes and portraying it how I saw it. And I think that's an important realization when you're building a multi-partner leadership team. Everybody has a different leadership style; for those who have a more charismatic nature, you have to be really careful that you're not always front and center driving the narrative when other people need to be doing it because then they'll never grow.

I probably was too timid during those times, and I could have said more things along the way to describe what I was thinking and why I thought this was interesting and a good idea. Normally, when I'm trying to understand what other people are thinking, I'll facilitate a conversation with everybody; they can say what they're really thinking, which might be, "I think this is a load of crap," or, "My world's going to blow up and I'm really scared." Let's get that out and process it as a team. I probably didn't do enough of that.

It's just so uncertain. And that's a lesson learned: to realize that it's uncertain throughout the whole process. Work authentically, communicate authentically, share your own vulnerability during the thing. Discuss with people that "I don't know if we should be doing this, but I'm going to continue the conversations, whatever they are."

Secrecy

Chris described that he regrets that when the sale of gravitytank was announced, he wasn't more active in helping people process the change. Christian from T3 described that, during the acquisition, very few people knew about it; in fact, for a large part of the sales process, only Christian and his CEO had any idea that it was happening at all. Maria, Matthew, and the Coopers all also mentioned the veil of secrecy above the sale process.

This is an almost ubiquitous part of the process, and one of the most emotionally draining. Imagine that you're going through the day-to-day activities of running your company—hiring, firing, problem solving, selling work, motivating teams—with a giant secret that will impact all aspects of your business! And it's hard to keep a secret like this, because people who have worked closely with you for a long time will notice changes. When I was going through this process, I found myself wound up all the time, constantly churning in my head over all the open and incomplete parts of the process. That makes it extremely difficult to be present during meetings and conversations, and it also made me pretty snippy; I had less patience than normal for pretty basic activities.

Why keep the process secret?

There are several big reasons for holding the acquisition close to your chest.

First, you'll likely be contractually obligated to keep it quiet through an NDA, and probably an NDA that's much more constraining and punitive than a normal one you may sign in the course of business. Your team is already limited in what they can tell the world, but that doesn't mean they'll follow that responsibility, and I've found that designers are some of the worst gossips. A breach of this form of NDA may do more than just break the deal—you may find yourself facing damages as a result of a leak.

Additionally, secrecy is a form of risk management. There are many things that can tank a deal, including public scrutiny, unplanned attrition, and client turnover. Imagine that your clients have formed a close bond with you and your design team, and recognize the benefits of working with a small group that they trust. What will happen when you become part of a larger group? Will they lose the personalized attention they receive? Will your rates change? Will they have to work with new leaders, and re-establish a working cadence? Clients may decide that the risk isn't worth it, and they may choose to move on or change their minds about future contract commitments. That's a problem for your revenue planning, and *that's* a problem for your valuation.

Secrecy also limits the anxiety within your team. Change can be scary, particularly change that might impact quality of life and compensation. They'll have questions, but for a good part of the process, you won't have answers to give them. That sort of ambiguity, on top of the already ambiguous nature of creative problem solving, can be really overwhelming, and in addition to the stress it will cause, it may directly lead to people leaving.

If you keep the process private, there's an unfortunate reality you'll have to face when the process becomes public: people will feel that they've been left out of something important (they have!) and didn't get to voice their opinions (they haven't!), and so it's highly likely that you'll lose trust from some of the team members. People who have been at your company for a long time will feel particularly disappointed and ignored, and people in leadership will start to question what being a leader at your company actually means, if they don't get to help make big strategic decisions like this.

Ways to manage secrecy

Several of the people I spoke with described ways they handled this disappointment or feelings of being left out. Perhaps the most common is through providing financial incentives to stay. This form of retention bonus is typically offered to employees at the end of their first year post-acquisition, but might extend even further than that. And often, these bonuses can be extremely large, even approaching their entire yearly salary. We'll talk more about the mechanics of retention agreements later, but suffice to say that the money can be a good incentive, but many creative people value other things even more than financial incentive. What about their role and impact? What about their autonomy? And what about the culture of the company? It's hard to ensure that these won't change, or will change for the better, particularly when you don't actually know that's true. No one I spoke with had a good solution for this problem, other than being honest and direct about intention.

Another way that founders managed the potential lack of trust as a result of secrecy was to open a decision-making inner circle slowly, but still prior to the acquisition. Sue and Alan Cooper broadened the set of people who knew about a potential acquisition before the deal was done. Sometimes, a buyer may actually ask for this, because they want to interview the extended leadership team. Often, this is because they are looking for a group who can manage the team if you, as an executive, were to leave.

Still another way to manage this was to abdicate a large portion of the deal to the next level of leadership, as Chris Conley explained. This certainly signals trust and a belief in the team's ability to execute. Of course, it also means that the team may do things you don't agree with. That's a leap that many founders aren't willing to take. This also signals to the buyer that you may not be fully investing in sticking around when the deal is over, which might not be your intention.

156

Max Burton, Who Founded Matter and Then Sold It to Accenture in 2017

Max's experience is an enviable tour of creative powerhouses. He's held leadership positions at Smart Design, Nike and frog, and then founded and sold his design company, Matter, to Accenture.

Tell me a little about how you started your own consultancy.

I was at frog design for about 4 years. I wanted to have a bit more autonomy about what I choose to do and not do, so I left frog and started Matter. I started the company with the thought, "I want to do what *I* want to do."

It was just me when I started. I had one employee after a few months, and then it rapidly grew to just shy of 30 people in five years. The speed of growth was definitely taxing, and was hard to manage. Murphy Freelen, a colleague I had previously worked with, became my business partner. She was managing a lot of the business and administration, and that allowed me to focus more on creative and strategy for the company. Vision, strategy, marketing, new clients—that kind of work.

Did you found the company with the intention of being acquired?

No; I never was actually intending to be bought. That wasn't my motivation when I started the company. However, some things I did made us attractive to a buyer. We had a great team, the right kind of clients, and a strong brand that was recognized and somewhat unique and identifiable in the mass of other design studios. It was standing out.

Our team was a mix of industrial design, interaction design, experience designers, information architecture, motion designers... It was really good, and we were always busy. And we had a great culture. I think that was the other thing that attracted and kept people; they wanted to work there. For example,

I'm British, and we had tea time each afternoon at 4:00. It's a nice moment to take a break and connect with each other.

Our positioning in the marketplace was quite appealing at the time (in early 2013), too: we were *designing for the connected world*. I think that resonated with a lot of clients. We very quickly became on the radar of design firms, competing against some of the other big firms here like Ammunition, fuseproject. We had a lot of physical/digital convergence projects for Samsung, Logitech and Disney.

What sparked the idea of the acquisition?

We were working with Carnival Cruise Lines, our biggest client. We were the primary creative partner for what was called the Medallion Experience, which was making a connected smart ship; we were working on the guest-facing side of the experience. There were about another six firms doing other parts of the project. One firm was all about film and TV, and they made a television series. There was a big engineering firm, software engineering, and an electronics engineering firm. There was a company in LA that was doing a lot of the animated work.

Fjord was working on the project, too. They were focusing on the employee experience. They said, "You can't have a great customer experience unless you have a great backend and happy employees with the right tools."

We were at CES in 2014, and Carnival Cruise Company took out one of these massive, entire block exhibits. I was at one of the parties, and the General Manager for Fjord here in San Francisco, Steve Boswell—who worked with us at frog—said, "Are you interested in some sort of 'joining us kind of thing'?" And I said, "We're certainly interested in the conversation."

Carnival was our bread and butter and was weighted quite highly in terms of the amount of work we were doing relative to the other work. I knew that work would end, and it would probably mean we'd have to shrink. I didn't want to have to do that to the team. So selling was a bit of a strategic decision. I wanted the team to go on and for everybody to have the chance to continue. And it seemed like a good idea from that perspective.

I had calls from their acquisition team, and it went from there. It was about a six to eight-month conversation for the deal to go through, and then we were part of Fjord.

It sounds like your reason for selling had to do with minimizing your risk and diversifying your client base. What do you think was their goal—why do you think Fjord and Accenture wanted to buy Matter?

To this day, I don't fully understand their strategy. I was literally told, "One of the reasons that we are bringing you in is because you, Max Burton, know how to be entrepreneurial, know how to grow a business, build a brand, hire the best people, and get the good clients." They told me, "We need you to bring some of that juice, mojo, into Accenture."

But I think they were mostly interested in having the Carnival Cruise Line client. After the acquisition, they were able to do some follow-on work, mostly software kind of stuff, that was amounting to tens of millions of dollars.

Their motivations for buying us were not very clearly spelled out to me, and I think they were not particularly straight about their reasons for buying the company. If they were straight in the beginning, and transparent and honest, things would've gone smoother because people's expectations wouldn't have been mismatched. When people think they're doing one thing and then they're doing another thing, it's very uncomfortable for everyone.

Did your team stay?

No. Most of the team left within a year. The really top people, people who knew that they could be commanding good salaries... There's a big difference between agency world and corporate world. People who like agency world like the fact that it's not a corporate environment. They want that freedom, they want that creativity. They want to work on different kinds of projects. They want that casualness that comes with the small design studio. It quickly became very apparent that Fjord was also losing its identity, its culture, and the mothership of Accenture was slowly absorbing them in and all the other companies they bought. The ways of Accenture, the ways of working, influenced everything.

I found out later that they actually had an internal project at Accenture to figure out why CEOs of acquisitions like mine were leaving at such a high rate. What happened to Matter was not unique; it was across the board with lots of companies they bought. They bought the companies, and then very quickly people left.

Here's an example. For me as a creative, I think good ideas can come from anybody. It could be an intern, it could be the CEO. It doesn't really matter. The idea is what's important, not your title and your position.

But at Accenture, these frigging high-level managing directors would waltz into the meeting room and start directing people. "Do this. Do that. Do that." Then they'd piss off for six hours, come back, and say, "No, that's all wrong. Do it all over again."

I would think, "What the fuck? You don't even know what design is." It's these people who are just talking heads wearing suits, walking around like they own the world. It's awful.

As a designer, your first and foremost motivation is to be creative and to be in service of people. That is the first thing, and then money follows. Whereas with Accenture, money is first and everything else is next. It's extremely money focused. They're a very profitable business, so what can I say? But, when I had my own company, I made very strategic decisions to take on startups that didn't make much money as clients, because I knew that it would build our portfolio and that we could put it on our website that we could use for marketing, which would lead to bringing in bigger clients. That kind of strategy, they aren't interested in that. If the deal size wasn't bigger than half a million, they were not interested. Some of our work was industrial design, and industrial design deals don't go that high. That meant we were essentially starved of work because of those thresholds.

How quickly did you and your team realize that the experience wasn't working the way you expected?

Honestly, it was shockingly fast. I think in the first six months I realized there's something going on behind the scenes that I wasn't privy to.

Some of my team pretty much immediately said, "This is definitely not for me." A lot of people had previously worked at Lunar, or had friends who worked at Lunar. Lunar had been acquired by McKinsey, and they all heard about how hard that was. They said, "This is another big firm coming to eat us up."

Others tried it, and said, "This is interesting, because I'd like to learn about service design. I'd like to mix with the other creatives and do more strategy." For some of my team it was a good move, and they stuck around. For others it was just, "I'm not interested in it." Very quickly those people left and just found other jobs.

How many people left?

Everyone got some kind of money, a retention bonus, after year one. But after that, I think we went down from 28 to 15 people, and by the time I left, it was probably just ten, eight, nine people.

Why do you think that is?

I mentioned earlier that I do tea time every day. When we started, one of the things they asked was, "What is one of those cultural things you'd like to bring over to Fjord?" I said, "Tea time. It's a thing we really love to do, and it's a great time for us to connect as a team, as people, just not about the work always." They said, "Okay. We're going to do that. We're going to bring that cultural part to the company."

After a year, we had this offsite. We asked the employees, "What is one of the most engaging, attractive things that you like about Fjord?" Almost everybody said, "Tea time."

But then, after that, the effort they put into it dwindled to nothing. They just used the facilities people, who brought a bunch of tea bags, and had hot water and some stale cookies. This is not culture building, this is culture destruction.

Did you see that sort of issue happening right away?

They left our brand alone for a year, but after one year they sunsetted it. Their belief was that I, personally, was the way to sell this type of work. I told them, "The brand I built is the means of generating work. You cut the name, and if you don't do something that's going to remarket the company somehow, we're just going to starve." We were just given work that was within the Accenture world.

Design is tiny compared to a big multi-year software deal, digital transformation deal, which is $100 million. Do they really care about a half-a-million-dollar program with design? No, not unless it leads to $10, $50 million.

And I understand that. They have a bar they all have to hit. When you get promoted in the Accenture system, you then have to close more and more millions of dollars of deals a year. I had to close $6 million in deals a year, which was really hard. So I spent my whole time trying to close deals, and 90% of them just fell through. It was very hard. Very, very hard.

What would happen if you didn't hit that number?

You would get fired. They hold your feet to the fire. It was such a complicated formula to determine how much I could say that I was responsible for closing business. So complicated; it doesn't encourage people to do it.

There were so many things that were just overly complicated and overly frustrating to do. When you have a small company, you don't have to jump through these hoops and hurdles.

Here's an example. Marriott is a big customer of Accenture, and I helped close a deal there which was a multimillion-dollar deal. I was part of the team that closed the deal. But I don't know how they figured out what percentage I got of that deal, what I got credit for. I don't even understand.

Tell me a little about the finances and the negotiations prior to the deal closing.

The deal was a mixture of an immediate payout—which, percentage-wise, was quite high—then it was payouts over three years, but it was also then dependent on how many of my team members left. If more people left, the less I would get.

Did you last those three years?

No. I left some money out. And there was another massive amount of money that would've been there if I stayed for five years, but I thought, "I'm not going to waste my life." I'm not a money-first person. I said, "I'm not going to sell my soul for five years."

Some of the work we were doing was very, very hard. I was on the plane all the time; I did 100,000 miles every year, and the expectations around the work style were really rough. Working until 3:00 in the morning, getting up at 6:00 in the morning to go fly to a client and present all day, and then get back on a plane and go to another. It was quite grueling. And even from a health perspective, it was really hard to do. I said, "I don't want to do five years here," so I left a lot of money on the table.

Did you feel like you knew what you were doing during the acquisition process?

Murphy, the partner I mentioned earlier, had some friends in the Bay Area who had already been acquired. They said, "Okay. You need to have a good M&A lawyer who represents you. You need to have, maybe, someone who's good on the accounting side." I hired these two people as consultants, and they were really helpful. We were able to raise the price through negotiations.

The deal itself was clear. The deal in terms of the things written on paper is one thing. It's very nuts and bolts. But if you're going to do this, you really need to go into a lot more detail. Have everything written down that you can. Everything should be crystal clear. Some of those are more like the soft things around culture, around working with startups, all of the things that are important for designers.

When we were working through the process, I negotiated a million dollars to use to do some strategic work or creative work with clients which would be brand building and fun for the team. But that million dollars somehow disappeared. It was a verbal agreement; I put trust in people. I probably should have had it in writing.

That's my guidance to any design firm that wants to be acquired. Ask for some of those things that may be a bit fuzzy but important to your team, important to you, important to the culture of the company.

Are you glad you made the decision to sell the company?

In terms of the financial structure, I don't really have complaints; I think it was fair. From a personal perspective, at that point in my life, it was probably a single moment to actually make a significant amount of money, and not be too worried about the future. Going into it, I knew that if I didn't like it, I would just leave and I could start again. It's not easy, but I could do it. But what pains me the most about the experience is about my team. I felt that I let them down a bit because I didn't know that it wouldn't be what I thought it was going to be. If I'd known, I would've done more to protect them. That's this frustration I have, and it's disappointing that I couldn't have protected them more.

It was a mismatch of expectations. I thought it was going to be one thing, and it ended up being slightly something different. And my team was not really that interested in it.

Some people were interested in service design, some people wanted to learn about business. Some people thought, "This is good learning. I'm going to do it for a few years and come out better on the other side." But, for a lot of people who I'd say are hardcore creatives, it wasn't the right environment for them. A lot of the really talented, intuitively good designers—they are inspired, and they put their heart and soul into things—said, "This is not me." Those are the people I feel I could have supported better.

I wish that I had more clarity around what was going to happen to my brand, my clients, and the ability to keep it going. Pretty much all the clients, as soon as we went to Fjord, asked, "Did Matter just go out of business? I thought you disappeared. It's just gone." Not the big clients, but a lot of the smaller clients said, "I just thought you must have closed shop."

And that's terrible. I put my heart and soul into building a brand and reputation in the Bay Area. Even today people say, "I remember Matter. They were doing some really great work, and you were a rising star in the Bay Area."

Losing Control of Your Brand

Max built a brand that was recognized as a top-tier agency; as he described it, the brand was beginning to play on equal footing as some of the more established consultancies. He felt that, after the acquisition, that brand disappeared. While he was certainly responsible for shaping the vision and tenor of the company, he recognized that his personal name was less important than the name of the company and the reputation that came with it. But that distinction wasn't clear to Accenture (or, they didn't care!) and so the brand Matter faded away.

Sue and Alan Cooper had a similar experience in losing the name of their company, and what that name signaled to the world, and it's easy to imagine how difficult it must be when your name is literally connected to the brand. They noted that when the company was fully integrated, the Cooper website was taken down, which has consequences: pride of ownership aside, people who previously worked at Cooper suddenly had no real evidence of that part of their employment history!

I chatted with another founder who named her company as a *portmanteau*—a combination of her name and her partner's name. The name didn't go away, but they no longer had control over what it represented. And I spoke with another founder who described that the feeling he felt after his sale was "mourning"—that he considered his brand to have died, and his feelings were couched in sorrow. His co-founders had their old logo tattooed on their bodies to make sure they never forgot what they built.

It's inevitable that your brand is going away, or going to change dramatically, at least in some respect. Hot Studio, gravitytank, T3, User Centric and Idean all evolved or disappeared, both in name and in their industry essence. Given the likelihood of this change, and the way the brand is connected to your heart and soul as a founder, there are a number of things to consider before selling.

Are you logistically prepared for your brand to disappear?

It's not easy to imagine the emotional impact of losing your brand, but it's even harder to imagine the logistical impact. If you are like the founders I spoke with, you've likely integrated yourself into your company in ways that were helpful and healthy in early parts of your entrepreneurial journey, but become really problematic when you go to separate yourself.

Your email address, logins and passwords

At some point post-acquisition, your old email address will stop working. In some cases, it will be forwarded to an address at the new company, but in many cases, it simply disappears: when people email you, their email will get kicked back as undeliverable. Imagine being on the other end of that one; a client you haven't spoken with in years is interested in working with you again, but when they send you an email, it bounces back. Is the company still in business? Did you get fired? They'll never know, unless they take a proactive step to track you down.

Your email address is your login to sites. When you can't remember your password, you get a "reset password" email with a link to click. What if you can't click it because that address doesn't exist anymore? Your email frequently acts as a form of two-factor authentication, with a six digit code sent to it to confirm you are who you say you are. What if you can't get the code?

It's inevitable that in the history of running your business, you've used your business email address for non-business activities. Before you sell your company, take the time to write down every site you visit that uses your business email address for personal activities—and then methodically change your email address to a personal account. If you use a password manager, this is a bit easier; if you don't, it's a time consuming and arduous process. But it's worth it, because post-acquisition, you might get locked out of your 401(k) or bank account!

Your contact list and email archive

My "inbox" is really a catch-all for every email I've ever received, and it has tens of thousands of messages in it. Most are useless, but I search those emails daily to find context for an old conversation, remind myself who a contact might be, or to dig up poorly archived or organized attachments and documents. It's a fundamental part of doing business, and when your email gets shut off, it's gone.

My contacts list works the same way for me. Without the ability to auto-complete an email address or track down someone's larger contact context, I'm lost. That, too, is gone when your email account gets shut off.

You can download your MBOX file, but it's probably in violation of your sale agreement; same with your contacts list. So before you sell your company, think long and hard about how tools like email and your digital calendar support you in your work. If you're committing to an earnout, your existing contacts and the things you've done for them in the past are critical to your success. Like everything else, if this isn't figured out and negotiated prior to a sale, you'll lose leverage—and therefore, urgency—in any sort of transition.

Are you emotionally ready for the history of your brand to disappear?

It's likely that the web is the primary source of historic information for your digital company. You have social media posts, microsites, thought-leadership content, blog posts, Vimeo videos, case studies, and more. When you sign those materials over to a new owner, they can do anything they want with them, including remove them entirely. Sue and Alan Cooper described that their former employees have no place to point prospective employers, as the Cooper site redirects to Designit (with no reference to the former company at all). As of this writing, Idean forwards to frog, T3 forwards to Material Plus, Matter is a dead link, gravitytank forwards to Salesforce, and so-on. The Wayback Machine has been generous to the content of these sites, but embedded functionality typically doesn't work properly, and while it acts as a nice archive, it's not the same as the ability to point to a real, working web property.

Interestingly, these same companies—Idean, Cooper, and gravitytank—all still have Twitter accounts that are inactive, but maintain their previous posts. This may even be worse than a consistent takedown, as it can appear to be sloppy marketing, and may signal that the company still exists, but their web presence is simply not functioning properly.

Are you ready for the history of your brand to change?

Even worse than having your brand disappear is *losing control of it*. But when you go through an asset sale, you're giving up the ability to control the way your creation is presented to the world. When the acquiring company wants to change—not simply remove—your brand messaging and style, they can. And if you remain emotionally tied to the way the brand looks, feels and sounds, you're in for a difficult time when someone else claims creative control over it.

This might mean that content you've created, like blog posts, are attributed to someone else (it's likely you assigned copyright to the new owner). It may mean that the details of the aesthetic, like color, type, and layout consistency, start to degrade from the webpage. And it might mean that things you don't particularly value, like in-page advertising, may suddenly start to show up. What can also be trying is that, semantically, your name is still associated with those materials. For many of us, our company brand is built on our reputation for good design. If someone searches for you on Google, or sees a reference to something you've done, chances are it will link back to the site that you no longer control. And putting it lightly, that may not look like what you want.

Negotiating for the brand

You have some ability to minimize these issues, because you can negotiate to keep your brand intact. As we've seen, you have the most amount of leverage prior to signing an LOI, and while brand isn't typically part of a letter of intent, it can be, because anything can be negotiated, depending on what you are willing to give in exchange. So, if you want to keep parts of your brand in place and under your control, that's the time to do it. Here are the things you might push for:

Retain ownership over the brand.

One way to ensure that your brand lives on is simply not to sell it. You might negotiate that, while things like your contracts and staff transition to the buyer, the brand itself doesn't. That's tricky, though, and gets fairly existential quickly: what actually *is* a brand? If you feel that it's a comprehensive representation of the company (including the brand, mark, website, social media, attitude, and so-on), that's an awful lot to carve out of a sale. In an acqui-hire, that can probably be negotiated: Hot Studio is still alive with the same pre-sale brand aesthetic and ethos, perhaps because Facebook only wanted the talent. But if valuation is tied to revenue, and revenue is based on your ability to sell, the elements of the brand are a huge part of your business development story. You'll give up valuation to retain that ownership.

Retain control, but not ownership, of the brand.

You could negotiate that the brand, mark, website, social media, attitude, and so-on continue to exist and operate independently, similarly to how the owners at Idean argued for a clause for no operational changes for a period of time. While this certainly lets your message and approach live on, it challenges a key nature of a strategic acquisition. The buyer may be looking to leverage your company's skills in a "better together" or "one stop shop" storyline to the market. It seems disjoint, then, to have two separate brands presented to customers in two separate ways. And as we saw with Idean, the independent operations only continued for a certain amount of time; the acquiring company had inertia towards integration, and after several years, the brand was absorbed.

Selective ownership or copyright assignment.

If you have a strong thought-leadership presence, you might want to argue to retain copyright over the materials that have been generated. A compromise may be to grant a free and perpetual license for the acquirer to *use* those items, but for you to use them, too. A buyer may have the most appetite for a proposal like this, but they'll view these items as intellectual property; again, giving up IP may mean giving up valuation.

Doreen Lorenzo, Who Was the CEO of frog design When It Was Acquired by Aricent in 2006

The last story we'll read about is from my conversation with Doreen Lorenzo. Under Doreen's leadership, frog drove an industry revolution in strategic design, a rise of design-as-innovation, and the acceptance of design as a broad creative power for social change. During her tenure as CEO, she helped the company survive economic downturns, established frog as a global brand, drove massive growth in revenue and staff size, and saw the company change ownership twice. And she also hired me!

Tell me a little about your experience at frog design.

I started at frog in 1997. Before that, I was the Head of Marketing at Power Computing, and I hired Virtual Studio—Mark Rolston and Collin Cole's company—to do our e-Commerce website.

At about the same time, Virtual Studio was acquired by frog. frog's founder Hartmut Esslinger had started to see that the digital future wasn't just about websites; he saw that products were starting to have digital interfaces and he needed people who understood digital. There weren't a lot of software digital interface people at the time. Hartmut found these guys in Austin, and they began to work with him on a couple of projects, and then he decided he wanted to buy them.

And *also* at the same time, Steve Jobs came back from NeXT to Apple. He said, "Licensing is dead," and he told us at Power Computing, "I'm going to buy your company or I'm going to put you out of business; I'm putting everybody else out of business." So he bought Power Computing.

Hartmut had been advising Steve about design, I was at Power Computing, frog bought Virtual Studio, and it all sort of came together. We caught the digital wave. I became the Chief Operating Officer of frog. And the company went gangbusters. We opened offices all over.

Then 2001 hit. It was dark. Hartmut and his wife and co-founder Patricia had invested a great deal of their own money into frog at that point, and when it went south, it went *really* south. They did a lot to keep frog alive, but we had to do tons of layoffs. And it was awful.

At the end, Patricia said, "I don't ever want to do this again." So in 2004, when they were approached by Flextronics about an acquisition, they took it. They sold 80% of frog to Flextronics and they basically backed away; they kind of handed me the reins to go run the company.

The whole point of the acquisition was that we were supposed to work with Flextronics doing hardware and software integration with their factories. It never happened. They never talked to us, and nothing happened. Fast forward to 2006; the CEO of Flextronics went to join the investment company KKR as a partner. He wanted to take all of these software companies that Flextronics had bought, including frog, and roll them into a business. KKR bought Patricia and Hartmut out entirely, and that new company became Aricent. I became president of frog, and from then until about 2012, they left us alone.

In about 2012, a new CEO came into Aricent, and they decided to try to integrate everything. They felt that's where the value was. But every time they would bring the subject up, I would fight them, and so they booted me out.

After I left, Aricent sold to Altran, and Altran sold to Capgemini, and that's where they are today.

It sounds like it all worked pretty well when the parent company—be it Flextronics or Aricent—left frog alone, but it started to fall apart when one company tried to integrate the other company. Why do you think that is?

One reason is the finances.

In managed services or IT services, you could have two years of visibility into a contract value. But in a creative services company, there's no visibility in growth. Innovation is not a line item in anybody's P&L. The work that you do requires almost constant delight, constantly proving to people that you can provide something that no one else can. They have to go and dig up money every quarter. This is how our industry worked, and it still works that way. That was really hard for financial people. Aricent was owned by a private equity company, and that's all they knew. They liked our output, they liked what they saw, and they liked the notoriety that the company got, but they couldn't understand the business model because it goes against everything that most financial people understand as good business practice. The sales cycles are long but short: it takes you a long time to get the sales opportunity, then it's a short sale, and then you've got to do it all over again. And that's really hard to understand.

They started to try to "fix it." Our overhead costs were higher and the margins didn't operate at the same margins that a lot of these integrators operate at. The margins that we had at frog were exceptional, but they still tried to improve them. Creative is so labor-intensive and people-intensive, and that's hard for financial people to swallow. So they tried to figure out how to operationalize creativity.

They told me, "We'll get rid of your finance team." But if you get rid of the finance team, you can't get things done fast. And in our industry, you've got to get things done fast. For example, sometimes we need to get on a plane and go to Cuba *today* to do that interview for a client. Well, in a large corporation, that takes a long time to do. We were at odds with each other, and so it became clear that they didn't understand what we did. That's where the mismatch happened. And it was incredibly frustrating, because I couldn't operate the way I always operated.

Another example was pricing.

In creative services, your pricing model is never really fixed; it's a very fluid pricing model. And it's really dependent on how much business you have at that moment or how much you can charge a client. It's about the value you are going to bring to the company through the project. And that model is just insane to some people. They would ask, "What do you mean you don't have a fixed pricing model?"

We *say* we have an hourly rate, but we don't really have an hourly rate. We kind of know what we have to make, and by managing the project, we can make a profit. That's why program management is so important. But it's not based on saying, "I'm going to bill you for 50 man-hours a month for the next 10 months." It just doesn't work like that.

Creativity doesn't have a fixed script. When you're coding for integration, there's a script. You know what you have to do. You know exactly the directions. It has steps. Creativity doesn't have steps. It's pretty messy and ugly. And if you're not really experienced at it, it can cost you your shirt. And if you don't know how to work with your clients to get them to feel comfortable about what you're delivering, you'll just go through these iterations over and over again.

Aricent couldn't understand that; it just didn't make sense to them. They wanted us to just give them the man-hours. But there's no such thing. You give the client a price and it's based on a whole bunch of particulars. By the time you get into the project, the particulars have already changed. You make mistakes when you get in the project. It's just a messy process. So what you try to do is bill enough to cover the mess. Nobody wants to talk about this; everyone wants to sound professional. But that's really how the creative industry works. We make a mess out there, and you hope that you have enough experience to be aware of the mess before it gets to be too much.

If you're a financial person, that's really scary. There's no visibility, and a lot of unknowns. They would ask, "How do you know the client is going to come back?" These integrators don't understand that it's the emotional things that bring clients back. If you do this right, your customer believes that nobody else can provide what you provide. That's how you keep people for years and years and years. You've created something nobody else can. It's that special.

These big tech integrators buy these design companies, and their EQ is really low. So the designers find themselves just painting pigs.

Why do you think these types of acquisitions don't work?

Nobody has figured out the connector. There's a connector between the shiny object of design and the backend drill work, but I have yet to see somebody make that connection work.

Part of it is culture. Software developers at these integrators don't think like designers. Designers don't mind the messy process. If the process isn't working, they'll tinker with it. But for software developers, they write code that has to be accurate.

This difference became a big problem for us. I would hear all the time that "We're not getting what we want and the work isn't good and the client's not going to be happy because we're not delivering." And the designers would moan and groan every time they had to go work with Aricent, because it was so hard. They just couldn't get what they thought they wanted.

And on the flip side, the IT people were like, "I don't know what you're talking about. You want something that doesn't make any sense to me."

All these design companies keep getting bought and bought and bought, but no one's bothered to say, "How do we do this? What would be the best way to do this? And what's the expectation once that happens?" I don't think anybody ever does the visioning exercises to say, "What is this going to look like when the acquisition is done?"

Everybody says the same thing: "We're going to leave you alone." But that doesn't make sense from a business perspective, and I understand that. If you're running a business and you have your own finance team and your own sales team, and I'm running my business with *another* finance and sales team, you're losing me money. Does that make sense? Why did I buy you?

When you started to see this happen at frog, what did you do?

I became a shield. The designers didn't know half of it; the company just went on as business as usual. But I came out of board meetings or business meetings bloodied from the fights. It was exhausting.

I left, and I heard that the person who was put in charge said, "Let's integrate." And that was the rude awakening. That's when Mark Rolston and a whole bunch of key people left. They said, "Well, we don't want to do this."

What could you have done differently up-front, before the Aricent acquisition happened, in order to ensure a better result and to retain more of your staff?

It's really about expectations of the goals of the acquisition, and figuring out how to connect these two very disparate pieces. Can we bridge that, or is there no bridge? There's always going to be change, and it isn't going to work like a fairytale. They aren't going to leave us alone or let us stay independent. That's not realistic.

You've got to figure out the human resources, which becomes a big issue. Human resources in a creative organization are very different from human resources in a software integrator. In a software integrator's organization, you're dealing with batches of thousands of students who come out of school each year. In a design organization, you're hiring the "bespoke, pick the daisy beautiful flower."

It's about culture. What is really the culture of the parent company? And is that going to overpower the culture of the design firm? Culture is about how we do the work. What's the ethos of how we work? How do we create an environment where we can create things? Those environments are hard. It's very difficult to have an environment where everybody's not afraid to create and come up with something. Oftentimes in these large organizations, you've got so many rules and regulations and other things that are influencing your success that you can't create. How do you protect that essence? Your KPIs for design will be very different from what a software person is doing.

Aricent's culture was revenue driven. Just totally revenue and EBITDA driven. It was all about profitability, growing the business, profitability. And these integrators, there's so many of them, and so the competition is fierce. There's no discernible way for them to stand out, so they're looking for something to make them differentiated. They think that's design, but when they try it, they get frustrated.

Do you think it's actually possible to do an acquisition like frog and Aricent and be successful?

I actually don't think it is. I don't think anybody's answered the hard question: what is that connector? And if you can't figure that out, accept that you're going to get paid a handsome sum for something you built, suck it up and then turn around and go build it again.

Cultural Collisions

Doreen described a collision between frog's creative culture and Aricent's Information Technology culture. This IT culture is typical of big system integrators, like Tata, Infosys, Cognizant, Wipro (who acquired Cooper), and Capgemini (who acquired Idean). These companies work on massive back-end system integration efforts, or installations of solutions like SAP or Oracle, or rollouts of Salesforce, and so-on. In these integration efforts, a focus isn't on creativity and innovation; it's on predictability, efficiency, and cost minimization.

Innovation is about making things the world hasn't seen before, and while those things can be exciting, they also carry a tremendous amount of risk. People who are comfortable with taking innovation risks are typically comfortable with ill-defined problems, organic processes, change, failure, and incremental improvement.

Integration is about doing things that are proven to work: following a tested, repeatable and rock-solid process. People who are comfortable with this type of rigid structure are usually equally at-ease when they have a well-defined problem, clear constraints and expectations, and most importantly, a clear view of a goal and a set of objective criteria upon which to judge success.

When a company full of risk-takers and dreamers crashes into a company full of operators and experts in efficiency, the cultural implications can be enormous. Similar words have very different meanings; "following a process" carries dramatically different implications to someone drawing storyboards as it does to someone responsible for a five-nines availability service-level agreement. And while these boundaries aren't rigid and people can change and adapt, there is inertia in both cultures towards *doing what they've always done, because it worked*. frog was acquired because they were good at being designerly. Aricent was in a position to acquire them because they were good at being efficient and effective. Expecting either of these organizations to change quickly seems silly and shortsighted.

A cultural collision doesn't just happen when design meets IT. Phil Barrett and Max Burton both described the way their agencies ran head-first into the world of operational consulting and accounting (as Phil described, "If you actually think about and ask, 'What's the matter here?' The matter is, if you've got an organization created by accountants, for accountants, operated by accountants, and you take those systems and try to apply them to design, they don't work very well. That's the truth of it").

And the culture clash is evident even when a creative company encounters another creative company! Christian talked about how LRW had made several acquisitions before T3, and when they began to integrate all of these creative companies, cultural differences crept up quickly. He attributed the difficulty in change to the fact that the founders of the various companies were still employed, still viewed their companies as "theirs," and still pushed the same approach and way of thinking that they had pre-acquisition. His example of title collision is a simple but clear way in which these issues manifest: if I'm an Executive Creative Director after 20 years in the business, and you're an Executive Creative Director after three years, we're bound to have an emotional reaction to the idea of working side by side.

When you start to think about selling your company, planning for a cultural collision is perhaps the most important thing you can do. You won't know exactly what you're in for before an "integration effort" begins, but these are some of the differences to expect:

The way you sell

Design problems are, by definition, always unique. As design agencies take on bigger and more complicated client problems, projects become more expensive, have higher internal visibility, and become perceived as riskier. That means that the sale cycle to close these deals becomes more individualized and more relationship driven. During the business development process, the sales team—typically, creative directors or, as described by many of these founders, the founders themselves—spend time to understand the unique needs of the clients and tailor a program to suit those needs and address those concerns.

That's entirely at odds with the way the design leaders I spoke with described how their parent buyers thought about sales. Phil explained that at Deloitte, his sales efforts became just a small part in a much larger deal; as he described, he would be asked to include design in an existing bid on a program because, "It'll make us look really good." He might not even have a chance to explain the value of his small bit of the proposal, because it would eventually be presented by someone else entirely. Matthew echoed that experience with Capgemini, where their sales team would say, "Hey, here's my spec sheet and I got all this stuff. Which ones do you want to buy?"

And, as Doreen described above, it's inevitable that a bigger company moves slower than a smaller company, but agencies are accustomed to responding to potential new business extremely quickly, because innovation budgets are rarely planned and may disappear as the company questions the risk and reward of creativity.

The way you work

Design is about dreaming. There's no right or wrong way to dream. And while design eventually becomes super pragmatic and practical, during an implementation phase or during sprint-work, it's still about creating things that don't yet exist, and there's rarely a playbook or a set of rote processes to follow; in fact, if there were, most designers would leave, because they would feel their creativity stifled. Creative directors see patterns over the course of their project experiences, but typically come to terms with the flexible and iterative nature of design.

But an IT rollout of Oracle—while always unique—is expected to be much more structured, planned, and contained. I don't know any IT project lead who would feel comfortable saying, "And then we'll synthesize requirements for a few weeks and draw; I'm not sure what will come out of it, but it will be pretty great." And the whole point of an IT install is to get it right the first time, not to hang out in the spin cycle of exploration.

There's also a fair degree of fuzzy-ness in staffing. The team that's specified for a project may need to change, and the bodies aren't interchangeable; while interaction designers may do some visual work, and visual designers may be conducting research or brainstorming strategies, craft really is specialized. Doreen explained that "Aricent couldn't understand that; it just didn't make sense to them. They wanted us to just give them the man-hours. But there's no such thing. You give the client a price and it's based on a whole bunch of particulars. By the time you get into the project, the particulars have already changed." Those particulars impact deliverables, and that changes the people and skills that need to be involved in the project.

This cultural class isn't just true with design and IT. I've observed a unique difference in the way operational consultants work and the way designers work, too. Different disciplines have tools that they gravitate to, because they are comfortable with them. Designers feel at-ease with drawing, and with digital tools that help them visualize things. Consultants from the "big five" are comfortable in Powerpoint and Excel, and so a designer may want to explore a problem visually while a consultant may want to explore it through financial modeling. In a perfect world, these skills complement one another. But in large companies with thousands of financial consultants, it's hard for a visual designer to find a voice or to be heard. Instead of making thoughtful and considered design solutions, they may find themselves, as Doreen explained, "painting pigs."

The way you bill and price

Sometimes designers bill hourly, but many design consultancies tie their rates to deliverables. When research has completed, they may invoice for research, and when the exploratory wireframes are completed, they may bill for interaction design. "Completed" is, like everything else in design, fuzzy; there's rarely an official acceptance or signoff of deliverables. Instead, the creative team and the client *feel* that a project is done.

That's just not how it's done in big strategy consultancies or IT integrators. Accenture and Deloitte are known to bill hourly, and an IT project has a pretty clear set of criteria for completion.

Additionally, costs are highly variable for designers. I don't know any design shop that bills by the wireframe, and while many shops have a unique bill rate based on the amount of experience a designer has, design agencies often find themselves fitting the cost of the project into the budget of the client.

Since many designers are driven by the experience of creating, I've seen agencies discounting their work tremendously, simply to get to do the project at all. I spoke with one design lead at Argo who said, only half jokingly, that he felt like sometimes he would think, "Just let me pay you to work on this, since it's so cool." Max echoed that sentiment; he wanted a carved-out budget to bring in client work that wasn't financially lucrative, but was fun for the team. The competitive and financially-motivated firms like Deloitte work in the other direction; as Phil said, the rate increase post-acquisition was "astronomical."

There's also a large difference that you'll likely experience in the mechanics of billing. This has less to do with the type of acquirer, and is instead based on size. In a small company, when it's time to invoice, you fire up Quickbooks and send an invoice. It takes 30 seconds, and there's no approval process, because the person sending it is probably you, the founder. But in a bigger company, you'll find yourself intertwined in big and often arduous IT systems.

The way you compensate and celebrate

During our first three years of operations, pre-acquisition, we took our team on vacation at the end of the year. We went to Costa Rica one year, Mexico another; it seemed fair that, after working hard, the partners shouldn't be the only ones to benefit. Additionally, we offered a revenue sharing program. At the end of each quarter, bonuses were based on how much money the company made, and these bonuses were relatively large.

Matthew explained that Idean took a company trip every year—once even taking everyone to Iceland. Chris Conley explained that they had a similar model at gravitytank; the company would wait until the end of the year to see how the finances looked, and then make decisions on how to share the wealth with the team.

These types of flexible rewards just aren't a common part of a large company, often for very logical reasons: they are too expensive to execute at scale. But spending is based on prioritization, and even at the scale of close to 1,000, Idean found a way to make it work. Pre-acquisition, it's entirely a question of what you value as a founder. Post-acquisition, it's entirely out of your hands.

Celebration is also not always about money. Max described that a small and inexpensive tradition of tea time disappeared, and that type of cultural ritual was something that tied the team together. I wouldn't think to put "tea time" in writing in a sale agreement, and you probably wouldn't either. But these are the types of small things that have big cultural impacts, and if too many of them change, you'll experience the cultural collision that ultimately led Doreen to leave frog.

Summary

You've just read ten interviews from leaders who have sold their design services companies. In addition to conducting these interviews, I've also had casual conversations with more than twenty other designers who have been in a management role during a sale process. And, in late 2021, my partners and I sold our design services company called Modernist Studio to a near-shore software integrator. We left in early 2023 (just 17 months later) to start Narrative; I can't speak of any of the details of my experience, but you can draw your own conclusions about how it went based on the simple fact that I wrote this book.

With all of the information I've learned, I've come to some pretty straight-forward conclusions.

Don't sell your company expecting that you'll be left alone to run it the way you always have. You won't. Matthew Robinson from Idean and Doreen Lorenzo from frog showed us that an acquirer can't help but make operational changes that have real impact on the business. You'll see changes in the small stuff, like time tracking and expense reporting, and you'll encounter changes in the big stuff, like the way you sell, the way you compensate your employees, and the way you spend your money. You'll encounter new processes and perspectives, and many times, those processes won't be "optional" and those perspectives are directives from your new senior leadership. You have complete autonomy in your company now. You won't once you sell it.

Don't sell your company expecting that you'll keep the culture of your company intact. You won't. Max Burton saw the meaningful rituals of tea time at Matter reduced to teabags and stale cookies at Accenture. Chris Conley explained that he walked away from a potential acquisition because the acquiring company wouldn't let them reward their employees in the way they had grown used to. Rituals and rewards are a big part of culture; it's inevitable that the acquiring company will change them, or remove them entirely.

Don't sell your company expecting that you'll leverage the sales pipeline and business-development team from the acquiring company. You won't. Christian described a completely contradictory sales process between T3 and LRW Group, where T3 leveraged relationships and LRW leaned on mass emails. Matthew Robinson explained that Capgemini used Idean's resources as tiny bits of larger deals: the revenue benefits went in one direction, only.

Don't sell your company and tie money to an earnout or retention agreement, expecting to control the result. You can't. Phil Barrett described a complex formula that defined who got credit for a sale, and he explained that he still doesn't really understand the details of the earnout—he even left early without realizing the duration he had committed to. After a terrible experience at Facebook, Maria Giudice left early, and left millions on the table. In the thrill of a sale, your future at a new company looks limitless. Reality kicks in quickly.

And *don't* sell your company thinking that verbal promises made to you will be held up. They won't. Max Burton talked about a million dollars that was allocated for brand building and to subsidize projects for his team that were less profitable but more fun. It wasn't in writing, and it didn't materialize. Gavin Lew expressed frustration on the lack of specification of what "counts" as recognized revenue. If it was in writing, it would have been clear. It's unlikely that the buyer is trying to lie or trick you. More likely, a verbal promise wasn't really thought out, wasn't really internalized, and—while it was important to you—wasn't important to the buyer, so they simply forgot about it.

There's really only one reason to sell your creative services consultancy.

The one reason to sell your creative services company is to make a bunch of money.

And if that's your goal, ***do it!*** You've worked hard to build something, and if you are at the point of time where you want to reap the financial benefits for you and your team, a sale is a great way to end an experience you should be extremely proud of. Sell the company, take the money, and walk away. Take some time off, write me a letter from the beach, and then—if you're up for it—roll up your sleeves and do it all again.

I'm sure there are design entrepreneurs who exited and can claim exceptions to these sweeping generalizations, and I say with all sincerity, *good for them.* They managed to bridge the divide between creativity and the inertia of M&A, which is a machine that seems to inhale innovation and exhale frustration, at least for designers.

I'm also sure there are entrepreneurs who would claim this summary as overly pessimistic. I don't think it is. I think it's *realistic.* You just read stories from people who have founded, ran, and sold some of the premier agencies in the world, and I don't feel I'm reading too much into their words in saying that many of them regret it.

As I reflected on everything I've learned, I kept returning to a sentiment that is better articulated by Phil Barrett, who sold his company to Accenture. This quote, which you previously read, is a wonderful summary of what it means to sell a design services company:

I learned that if you're sure that you want the money, and you are happy to let go of the asset, and you don't want the asset anymore... it's like, "I have had enough of running this fucking agency, I don't want to do it anymore, and I definitely am prepared to exchange all of that for some money and some heartache," then fine.

But if secretly, actually, you love what you do, then chances are you'll sell it to somebody else who doesn't get it. Because almost by definition, if they're trying to buy it off you, they don't get it, because they couldn't do it themselves. And if you love what you do, then you probably should carry on doing what you love.

The Acquisition Checklist

Each of the leaders I spoke with had unique experiences, but as you can tell, there's similarities in each acquisition that lead to a pretty crisp, clear set of heuristics for considering and preparing for a sale. These are the things to do as you entertain the idea, and as you go through the long, arduous process:

Identify why you are selling your company.

What a silly thing to have to remember to do, but how easy it is to skip: ask yourself why you are selling your company, and be honest in your answer. And then, as a constant reminder, write down your goal for the acquisition, put it on the wall, and live with it for a while.

I'm considering selling because...

- I'm bored and want a new challenge.

- I want the money.

- I'm ready to retire.

- I'm sick of some of the existing parts of running the business.

- I want to expand our sales pipeline.

- I want to grow the size of the team.

- I no longer want to be anxious about, or responsible for, payroll.

- I want to complement or grow the team's skillset.

- I want to be part of something bigger.

Plan your time.

Before you begin the process in-depth, create a plan for how your time will be spent; in the plan, address these points:

- Ensure the plan covers at least six months, and plan for a year
- Assume that you will need help: it will be really hard for you to run your business and work through the process at once
- Plan for the most time during the diligence process

The *form* of the plan isn't important—it can be bullet points on a list, post-it notes on your wall, or a written narrative—but you can start by answering questions like this:

What are the things I do right now in the business that take up the most time?

- Who will do those things if I don't have time?
- Will they need to know about the potential sale process?

What are the things I do right now that no one else can do?

- What will I sacrifice in order to keep doing those things while simultaneously dedicating myself to the sale?
- What are initiatives or activities I can back away from during the process, in order to free up more time?

What are trips or vacations that I have planned during the next 6–12 months?

- Can these be canceled or postponed?
- Will these events still be valuable or pleasurable if I'm on the phone or computer for a large part of the time?

What are things I do outside of work that take up the most time?

- How can I carve out time for my friends and family?

- How can I carve out time for my hobbies, activities, or things that I find relaxing and calming?

Create an advisory team.

You'll need a team to support you in the process to advise on and handle specific topics, many of which are topics designers typically stray away from. Include people to cover these roles, and if you don't already have people in your network like this, ask these questions as you recruit or hire them:

A banker

- Have you worked on acquisitions before?

- Have you worked on acquisitions of *service companies* before?

- Have you worked on acquisitions of creative design studios or agencies before?

- Do you have references from prior sales who I can talk to?

- Who will be working on my sale?

- How much time will I have with a partner, vs a junior associate?

- What multiples are you seeing in my industry?

- Who are some of the companies you will introduce me to right away?

- What is your compensation fee structure?

- Can you give me an example of how much I'll end up paying you based on various scenarios?

A law firm

- Have you worked on acquisitions before?

- Have you worked on acquisitions of *service companies* before?

- Have you worked on acquisitions of creative design studios or agencies before?

- Do you have references from prior sales who I can talk to?

- Who will be working on my sale?

- What are your fees?

- Are any fees tied to the success of the sale?

- Are any of the fees percentage based, rather than fixed?

- How will I communicate with you?

- How will you communicate with my banker or M&A advisor?

A CPA

- Have you worked on acquisitions before?

- Have you worked on acquisitions of *service companies* before?

- Have you worked on acquisitions of creative design studios or agencies before?

- Do you have references from prior sales who I can talk to?

- Have you worked through tax implications of M&A compensation structures?

- Have you worked with earned-out money?

- Have you worked with earned-out stock grants (in a public or private company)? Are you familiar with the IRS's 83(b) and other related laws and rules?

- Have you worked with the tax implications of Safe Harbor/Nexus?

Other founders

- Can you share the terms of your deal?

- Are you happy you sold?

- What multiple was your company valuation based on?

- What do you wish you had done differently?

Interview the potential acquirer, extensively.

You'll never really understand a company culture until you find yourself in it, but you can get to know the people you'll be working with by interviewing them as much as possible.

I would recommend these explicit interview steps to include, likely after the LOI is signed but before getting too far into diligence.

Do a project with the management team.

It doesn't need to be a complete client project, although that would be great; any project where you make things together will help you see how people think and act in a collaborative session. Some potential projects might include:

- Workshop the integration plan together.
- Brainstorm how the sales teams or business development processes will integrate.
- Co-sell something (either for real or hypothetically) where you both work on a pitch together.

In all cases, consider using your designerly process, which probably includes collaborative sketching, dreaming, externalization, and deep dives that last more than an hour. Look for clues about how the acquirer acts during these meetings, and consider checklists like these:

Who showed up?

- Did the executive team make time for the meeting?
- Were they really present, in mind, body, and spirit?
- Did they include other people, like their directors or star players?
- Did your potential new boss show up? Do they know who that is yet?
- Did they come in person?

How did they behave?

- Did they arrive on time?
- Did they help plan the session?
- Did they make things, and draw, and get hands-on?
- Did they close their laptops and turn off their phones?
- Did they ask questions?
- Did they make statements?
- Did they dedicate a material amount of time?
- Did they take responsibility for next steps or meetings to follow?

How did you feel?

- Were you intimidated?
- Were you supported?
- Did you feel like one team? How long did it take to feel that way?
- Did you feel equal?
- Did you sense optimism and potential?
- Did you feel heard?

One thing to try to observe during meetings with leadership is how people react to conflict or challenge. Push back (nicely!) on things they say, or question the root of their assertions; see how they respond. Find ways to provoke a rainy-day interaction, so you can see what happens when people aren't on their best footing.

A big clue about how you'll interact with a potential new management team will be how much time they are willing to give you. If the best they can do is a one-hour Zoom call, you can infer how difficult it's going to be to get their attention when you really need it.

Learn about the details of operations.

Since small, day-to-day interactions will have large impacts on sentiment, I would recommend doing your best to understand the details of what you and your team will experience by way of operations. Ask to speak with someone who can describe the mechanics of how their company runs, and consider prompting conversations around these questions:

What software is used, and what is the process, for...

- Invoicing clients
- Paying employees
- Submitting expense reports
- Requesting time off
- Tracking P&L
- Viewing quarterly financial progress
- Viewing accounts receivable and status of payment
- Requesting new software for your team or yourself
- Installing things on your laptop
- Getting new or replacement hardware
- Buying furniture for the office
- Buying supplies

- Training, both required and optional
- Giving raises
- Hiring & firing

Find out about approvals—what's the process, who's involved, how many people have to sign off, and how long these things take.

Make sure to learn about the different costs that you may not have been expecting, by asking things related to shared-services or overhead:

Will my business unit or team incur costs related to...
- Required training, such as harassment or safety education
- IT purchases, both for staff (laptops, monitors) but also infrastructure (internet, cloud storage)
- Food, beverages, snacks, and supplies
- Human Resources, Financial Services, and other fundamentals of running the business
- Facilities, including maintenance and upkeep, but also the basics: utilities, furniture, cleaning

Talk to the people who do the work.

Make an effort to drop below the C-suite or executives and interview the people who actually do the project work. If the company already has designers, find some time with them. Try to ask questions about:

What are projects like?
- What are you working on right now? Can I see it?
- Who is involved in defining, selling or scoping the work?
- Who do you work with on a daily basis?
- What software and hardware do you use? How do you feel about it?
- How long are your projects? Is that enough time?

- Do you have formal ways to get project feedback or criticism?

What's the management team like?

- Who is your manager? What are your interactions with them like?
- How frequently do you interact with the "skip level"—people one title or jump above your manager?
- If you asked the company management what you do, what would they say?

Negotiate hard up-front.

Before the LOI is in place, make sure you've pushed for the things that matter. Make sure you reflect on these things to see if they are important, and if they are, treat them as "first-class citizens" for negotiation, and *get them in writing*.

Reflect on hard and soft constraints.

How much control are you really willing to give up? Consider these constraints, and work through the implications of your answers:

What are the constraints you'll put on the deal during negotiation?

Yes / No / Negotiable	Ending the various experiences or traditions that we've established as a culture
Yes / No / Negotiable	Being unable to start another consultancy for a minimum of _____ year/s after leaving the new company
Yes / No / Negotiable	Being unable to recruit or work with your existing team for a minimum of _____ year/s after leaving the new company
Yes / No / Negotiable	Being unable to recruit or work with your existing clients for a minimum of _____ year/s after leaving the new company
Yes / No / Negotiable	Having a minimum of $_____ set aside as a discretionary budget per year

	What are the constraints you'll put on the deal during negotiation?
Yes / No / Negotiable	Receiving a minimum of $_____ in cash up front
Yes / No / Negotiable	Working for a minimum of _____ year/s at the new company
Yes / No / Negotiable	Having my money tied to the retention of my team
Yes / No / Negotiable	Giving a minimum of $_____ retention bonuses to my team, which might come out of my own share of the sale
Yes / No / Negotiable	Having my money tied to revenue that I need to sell
Yes / No / Negotiable	Having revenue defined as _____
Yes / No / Negotiable	Having my money tied to profit that I need to generate
Yes / No / Negotiable	Having profit defined as _____
Yes / No / Negotiable	Giving up control to hire, fire, provide bonuses and raises at will
Yes / No / Negotiable	Giving up control of the culture of my company
Yes / No / Negotiable	Using buyer-procured technology, which may include spyware or trackers
Yes / No / Negotiable	Having my team resourced to projects outside of my control

Be clear about worst-case scenarios and termination.

Work through these scenarios with your lawyer, and make sure you're clear about what happens in each case; what happens if...

- I'm fired for no reason?
- I'm fired for a legitimate reason?
- I'm let go during a layoff or staff reduction?
- The company goes public?
- The company is sold to another company?
- There's a reorg and I'm moved into a different business unit?
- I'm given a new manager?

- My title changes, and it is considered a demotion?

- My budget is decreased, or taken away entirely?

- My team is taken away from me, laid off, or fired?

Get your documents organized.

When you get to diligence, you'll have to produce a large quantity of documents. Here's a checklist of the things you'll need to gather (at a minimum):

Organization

A buyer will look for:

- Certificate of Filing with the state

- Operating Agreement

- Any documents related to stock or equity

- Company minutes for the last three years

Contracts—SOWs

A buyer will look for your SOW documents and a summary of the materials:

Client	Client name
Project	Project name and description
Date Signed	Date of signature
Duration/End Date	Start and end date of project
Payment Terms	Financial terms that override MSA defaults

Contracts—MSAs

A buyer will look for your MSA documents, signed, as well as a summary of the materials:

Client	Client name
Date Signed	Date of signature
Date Expires	Date of expiration, previous or future
Assignable?	Can the contract be assigned to the buyer as a result of the transaction, with or without approval from the client?
Non-Competes?	Does the MSA reference specific clients by name that the buyer will not be able to work with?
Default Payment Terms	Are there terms across all contracts?

Invoices

A buyer will look for your invoices, as well as a summary of the materials:

Invoice Number	Unique invoice number
Client	Client name
Project	Project name and description
Date Invoiced	Date the invoice was sent
Date Due	Date payment was expected
Received Date	Date payment was received, if any
Amount	Total amount of invoice

Financials

A buyer will look for:

- Three year trailing documents, including reconciled P&L, bank statements, payroll per employee, tax returns for company, tax returns for owners if the company is an LLC (and sometimes even if it isn't), and utilization reports for employees by employee, month, and client

- 18 month forward-looking P&L

- Accounts receivable and aging summary

- Insurance COIs

Human Resources

A buyer will look for:

- Signed employee agreements from the last three years

- Signed contractor agreements from the last three years

- Documents of all benefit programs offered to employees

- Documents of all policies, such as privacy, sexual harassment, etc.

Leases & inventory

A buyer will look for:

- Signed lease agreements for any facilities

- A list of all physical assets, primarily focused on furniture and computer hardware, along with depreciation schedules

- A list of all digital assets, such as website URLs

Put these items in a single place (Dropbox, Google Drive, etc.), and track them in a spreadsheet, so you'll be able to produce them quickly and without the added anxiety of organization during negotiation.

Make an integration plan.

Every single person I spoke with who had a negative sale process attributed it, in small or large, to the lack of a clear plan for integration. I would recommend working in close collaboration with your buyer to create a plan that includes all of these things (which are, basically, every part of the business!):

Organizational

What will change?	What will not change?	When will the changes happen?	Who is responsible for managing the changes?
Titles of your team members			
Salaries of your team members			
Reporting structure			

Clients and Contracts

What will change?	What will not change?	When will the changes happen?	Who is responsible for managing the changes?
Business development team integration			
Day-to-day client leads for existing programs			
Day-to-day client leads for new programs			
Buyer's access to your clients			
Your access to buyer's clients			
How you write, negotiate, and sign contracts			
Your ability to access legal support			
MSA and SOW templates			

Creative Services

What will change?	What will not change?	When will the changes happen?	Who is responsible for managing the changes?

What you sell

How you sell it

How you talk about your capabilities

How much your services cost

How many people work on a project

What types of people work on a project

Technology Operations

What will change?	What will not change?	When will the changes happen?	Who is responsible for managing the changes?

The hardware you use, and how you source it

The infrastructure in your office

The creative software you use, and how you source it

The operations software your team will use (for expense reporting, requesting time off, etc.)

The operations software you will use (for financial management, tracking performance, etc.)

People Operations

What will change?	What will not change?	When will the changes happen?	Who is responsible for managing the changes?

How you recruit and advertise for new talent

How you make an offer to a candidate and negotiate their terms

How you onboard new employees

How you manage performance issues

How you compensate, and how much you compensate

The ways you can reward strong effort or performance

Training and education

How you terminate staff

Policies related to time off, holidays, and other perks

How you bring on a contractor

Budgeting and Spending

What will change?	What will not change?	When will the changes happen?	Who is responsible for managing the changes?

How budgets work

When budgeting cycles happen

How you make small purchases

How you make large purchases

How you make crazy purchases, like sending the whole company on vacation

Facilities

What will change?	What will not change?	When will the changes happen?	Who is responsible for managing the changes?

How snacks, drinks, and other conveniences are selected and ordered

Where you office from

Who pays the utilities, and how

Brand

What will change?	What will not change?	When will the changes happen?	Who is responsible for managing the changes?

Your website

Your social media presence

The company name, mark, aesthetic, and identity

Be skeptical of the phrase "we'll figure it out later," and scenario-play the most important changes, to really think through how a change will work and feel.

Most importantly, write this integration plan down. And if parts of it are critical to your success, make those parts (or the whole thing) legally binding by including it in the sale agreement.

Take care of your team.

Most of the people I spoke with intended to take care of their team, but didn't feel that they did enough to ensure that their employees and colleagues were treated with the respect they deserved; some expressed regret related to both financial and cultural outcomes. Here are some of the things you can do to ensure you take care of your team:

Carve out money for retention.

Even if you haven't explicitly tied your personal compensation to the retention of your team, you'll want them to stick around. When things get rough, you'll need a way to motivate them, and while money isn't everything, it can sometimes be enough to get you through a rough transitional period. Recall that a number of the stories you've read mentioned money that was promised but disappeared; you won't be able to procure raises, bonuses, and an explicitly retention budget unless you argue for it up-front.

Give your team enough time to understand what's happening, and help them process the change.

The secrecy of the sale process often ends in an abrupt announcement, after the sale is concluded. But imagine being on the receiving end of that; yesterday, you worked at one company, today, you work at another, and you had no say in the matter. The longer you can provide your team to come to terms with the change, the better. If you can bring a larger group into the conversation early, do it; as Chris Conley described, he actually handed the transactional reins over to his trusted team. In addition to signaling trust, this gave the team much longer to better consider the implications of the change and get ready for it.

There is typically a large announcement to the company after a deal closes, and then the team attempts to go back to business as usual. But it's not usual, and a single meeting will not be enough for people to process the change. Hold multiple meetings to discuss the transaction, even weeks or months after the change has been initially communicated. Conduct small group meetings with key players from both your company and the buyer's company, so they have opportunities to get to know one another. Anticipate the animosity that Maria described at Facebook, and do your best to head off cultural differences by creating social events for both teams to experience at once.

Above all, try to remind yourself that, while you've been living the realities of the transaction for almost a year, your team is brand new to the change. They need more than a day, or a few hours, to get to try on the idea.

Be honest about ups, downs, unexpected events.

Change is scary, and while it's beneficial to verbally champion the new buyer, it's also valuable for people to explore a more tempered reality; designers are particularly good at seeing through a veil of optimism. This means being clear about some of the trepidation you had and may continue to have, and describing the real risks and challenges that are on the horizon. Every person I spoke with described that the integration is going to be hard (or downright impossible), and that's a good place to start this form of honest and earnest conversation.

Take care of yourself and your loved ones.

If you've thoughtfully made up your mind to go down the process, it's important to take care of your mental and physical health. You can't make rational decisions if you're a ball of anxiety, and the long hours of screen-time will take a toll on your body. And if you have family and friends supporting you, they'll absorb your emotions, too. This process will eat you up if you let it. So, I would recommend you:

1. Do something physical. If you go to the gym, keep going. If you run, keep running. And if you don't do any of these things, this is a pretty good time to start.
2. Go outside. Nature has a way of resetting anxiety. There's a Ralph Waldo Emerson quote that I've found captures this beautifully:

    In the woods... a man casts off his years, as the snake his slough, and at what period so ever of life, is always a child. In the woods, is perpetual youth... In the woods, we return to reason and faith. There I feel that nothing can befall me in life—no disgrace, no calamity.

3. Keep an eye on the drinking. If you find yourself on a roadshow, you'll be doing a lot of dinners, and a lot of happy hours. If you're a drinker, you'll see it ratchet up here, and I know I'm not on my A-game when I'm hung over.

4. Share details with your partner, if you have one. I'm not sure my wife really cared about the nuances of my SG&A forecast, but I know she felt happy about being included at that level of detail. It may be the last thing you want to talk about over dinner after thinking about it all day, but it will go a long way.

5. Set expectations about "do not disturb" hours with your team. My lawyer was great, and she stayed in constant communication with me. That meant I was getting texts at all hours of the night. It became important for me to be proactive in letting her know, "You won't be getting a response from me quickly at these times of day," so she wasn't left waiting at a critical moment.

Put these things on your calendar or to-do list, or you won't do them. Even hobbies that you regularly engage in will take the back burner as the excitement and anxiety of the deal progress. Make these things "first class citizens" in the context of your day.

The End to End Acquisition Journey

Selling	Valuing & Negotiation

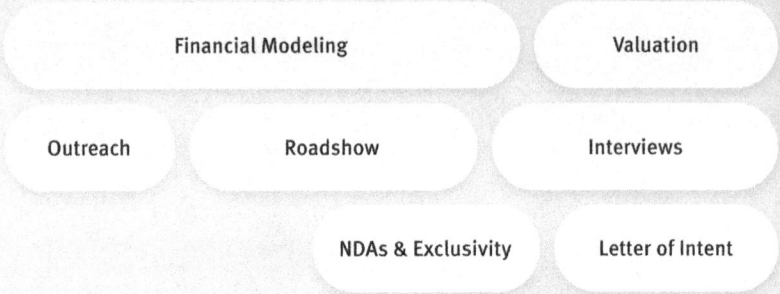

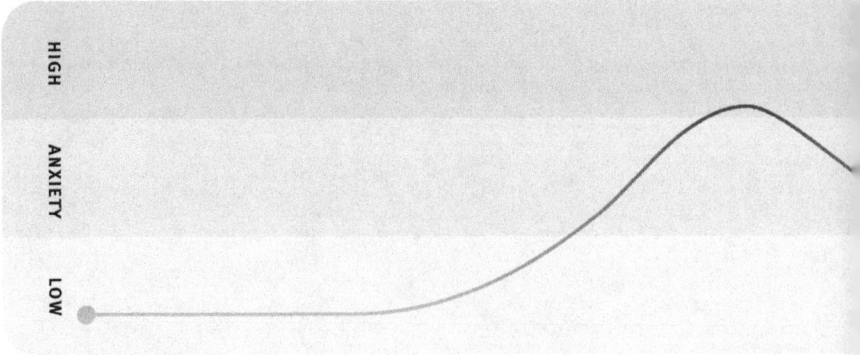

Financial Modeling

Valuation

Outreach

Roadshow

Interviews

NDAs & Exclusivity

Letter of Intent

● WORK ○ WAIT

HIGH

ANXIETY

LOW

Diligence

Closing

Purchase Agreement: Legal Negotiations

Quality of Earnings

Signatures

MSAs & SOWs

Payment

Invoices & Finances

New Employment

Team Interviews

Team Communication

Integration

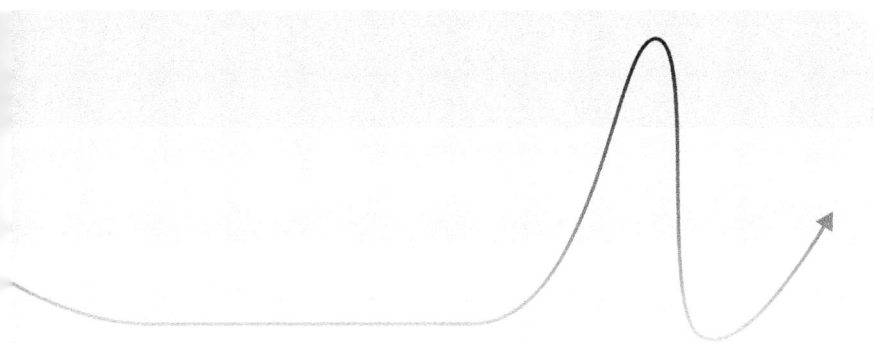

Example Letter of Intent (LOI)

This is an example of a Letter of Intent. Each LOI is very different, but this should give you a sense for the type of language that's used.

Overview

In this Transaction, the Seller will sell all of its assets to the Purchaser, except for cash, bank accounts, and any excluded assets that they both agreed upon. The Purchaser will only take responsibility for non-past due accounts payable included in the working capital adjustment and obligations for future performance under all assumed contracts, leases, and licenses (known as "Assumed Liabilities"). All other liabilities, such as indebtedness, tax liabilities, capital leases, change of control payments, severance payments, obligations to equity holders and benefit plans, transaction expenses, and any other liabilities, will be excluded and discharged by the Seller and its equity holders, and referred to as the "Excluded Liabilities."

Purchase Price

The Enterprise Value (EV) of the business, assessed on a cash-free debt-free basis, is $VALUATION, as evaluated by the Purchaser. To acquire the Purchased Assets, the Purchaser will pay the Purchase Consideration, which is calculated by adding the Enterprise Value to (i) any remaining cash and cash equivalents on the balance sheet at the Closing, if there are any, and (ii) the difference between the closing working capital and the negotiated target working capital, if greater or less.

The Purchase Consideration is divided into three parts: (a) $AMOUNT million in cash to be paid at the Closing, known as the Closing EV, (b) $AMOUNT million contingent on the financial performance during the Earnout Period, which lasts for 12 months until DATE, known as the Earnout, and (c) $AMOUNT million reserved for a management pool for non-member employees. The management pool will be paid out in full at the end of DATE, subject to continued employment. However, if an employee does not stay employed until DATE, their allocated portion of the management pool will be forfeited and not redistributed to anyone else. The specific allocation of the management pool will be determined and specified at the Closing.

Earnout

The Earnout will be earned as follows:

$AMOUNT will be earned at FIRST CALENDAR YEAR DATE if the Earnout EBITDA (defined below) for the calendar year ending DATE reaches $AMOUNT million or more. If the Earnout EBITDA is less than $AMOUNT million, the DATE Earnout will be zero.

$AMOUNT will be earned at SECOND CALENDAR YEAR DATE if the Earnout EBITDA (defined below) for the calendar year ending DATE reaches $AMOUNT million or more. If the Earnout EBITDA is less than $AMOUNT million, the DATE Earnout will be zero.

The calculation of "Earnout EBITDA" will be based on the net income of the Seller business unit, determined in accordance with generally accepted accounting principles that are consistently applied. This will be calculated by restoring amounts deducted for interest on borrowed money, taxes on income, depreciation and amortization, and by deducting all extraordinary items of income, interest and investment income, and gains on any sale or similar transaction that is not in the ordinary course of business. Purchaser will provide monthly financial reports for the Seller business unit, including revenue, operating income, net income, and EBITDA. The definitive documents will have standard review, payment, dispute resolution provisions, and a senior debt subordination agreement. Any Earnout that is due will be paid to the Sellers no later than 30 days after the end of the review period following the completion of a final independent auditor's report on the consolidated financial statements for DATE.

Working Capital

The Definitive Agreements will incorporate a working capital adjustment to the Enterprise Value, which will be estimated at Closing and reconciled post-closing. This adjustment will be based on the positive or negative difference between the target working capital and the closing working capital. The determination of the closing working capital will be in accordance with GAAP and Seller's historical accounting practices that were used in the preparation of the latest financial statements, without considering any purchase accounting resulting from the Transaction, as long as they are consistent with GAAP.

Escrow

Upon the Closing, the Purchaser shall deposit an amount of $AMOUNT in cash into an escrow account, known as the "Escrow Amount," which will be held for 12 months after the Closing, referred to as the "Escrow Term." The release of the Escrow Amount will be subject to the provisions of the Escrow Agreement. During the Escrow Term, any indemnification obligations of the Sellers shall be satisfied initially by reducing the principal amount of the escrow.

Fees

The Seller is responsible for paying any brokerage fees and commissions. The Purchaser will bear all its expenses, such as legal, accounting, consulting, financing, and other fees and out-of-pocket expenses. Unless otherwise stated, no fees related to the transaction or post-closing will be charged.

Conditions to the Purchaser Obligations to Close

The completion of the transaction by the Purchaser and Seller will only be subject to the following conditions precedent:

(a) Sellers performing the covenants in the Purchase Agreement;

(b) Sellers' representations and warranties being true in all material respects on the closing date;

(c) No court or regulatory order preventing the parties from completing the transaction;

(d) Obtaining consents to change of control for material contracts containing change of control clauses;

(e) No material adverse change affecting the Company, except for any changes that are not specific to the Company; and

(f) Sellers and Purchaser satisfying all closing delivery requirements under the purchase agreement.

The purchase agreement will not include any financing or due diligence conditions.

Representations

As part of the Definitive Agreements, Seller and each of the Sellers will provide customary representations and warranties for a transaction of this nature. These representations and warranties will remain in effect for 12 months following the Closing, except for the Fundamental Reps, which will survive indefinitely after the Closing. Fundamental Reps include representations and warranties related to due authorization, no-conflict, validity and enforceability, capitalization, affiliate transactions, title to assets, and brokers. Tax matters will survive until 90 days after the expiration of all applicable statutes of limitations (including all extensions thereof) related to the underlying subject matter being represented.

Indemnities

Sellers shall indemnify Purchaser, based on the terms and conditions outlined below, for (a) any violation of representations and warranties described in the Definitive Agreements, (b) any violation of covenants provided in the Definitive

Agreements, (c) any Excluded Liabilities, (d) any pre-closing tax obligations, and (e) claims arising from fraudulent representation in the Definitive Agreement. Such indemnification will be on a several basis, pro rata share, and not joint and several among the Sellers.

Liability

For all representations, warranties, indemnities, and other obligations provided by the Sellers regarding the Company, each Seller will be separately liable (and not jointly and severally liable). For all representations, warranties, indemnities, and other obligations provided by a Seller regarding themselves, each Seller will be separately liable (and not jointly and severally liable).

Sample Diligence Requests

This is a list of documents and information you may be asked for during diligence.

Employee Benefits

All corporate policies, manuals and employee handbooks

All employee benefit, pension, health, deferred compensation, bonus, profit-sharing, equity appreciation, option grants or severance arrangements or plans

Collective bargaining and other labor agreements, together with a description of any significant labor problems or union activities that the Company has experienced including human rights or similar complaints

Description of management loans (if any)

Employee and independent contractor census chart that includes the current salary/wage rate, exempt/non-exempt status, job function and part-time/full-time status

Employment, consulting, severance or other similar agreements

Form of confidentiality, non-competition, non-solicitation and/or invention agreements for employees

Indemnification agreements (if any)

All employee benefit, pension, health, deferred compensation, bonus, profit-sharing, equity appreciation, option grants or severance arrangements or plans

Contracts

Agreements under which the amount payable by Company is dependent on the revenue, income or similar measure of Company or any other person or entity

Agreements with any governmental entity

Agreements with respect to mergers, acquisitions or divestitures

Agreements with respect to which Company has any liability or obligation involving more than $50,000, contingent or otherwise

Agreements with retailers, distributors and re-sellers

Agreements with the Company's important vendors and suppliers, including Agreements with respect to (i) hosting or co-location facility services and (ii) providers of services or products that the Company resells

All affiliate or inter-company contracts and arrangements (including directors, officers, investors and family members, including any entities owned or controlled by the foregoing)

All other material contracts not provided in response to the above

Strategic alliance, OEM, channel partner, joint development, joint research, joint venture, partnership or similar agreements

Agreements that place any material limitation on the business of Company or that contains any exclusivity, "most favored nation," non-competition, non-solicitation, price restriction, right of first refusal or similar provisions

All agreements with the Company's important vendors and suppliers, including all agreements with respect to (i) hosting or co-location facility services and (ii) providers of services or products that the Company resells

Facilities

All documents relating to leased property (personal or real)

All documents relating to real property owned by the Company (if any)

All documents relating to physical property (personal or real)

Finances - Overview

All documents relating to securities including (a) the voting, purchase, repurchase, issuance, registration or sale thereof and (b) all documents related to any prior financings involving a Company

All Section 409A reports and other appraisals of the Company's securities

Detailed capitalization table listing the current holders for each series and class of security, including options, warrants and equity appreciation rights

Warrants, options, convertible notes and any other rights to acquire securities

Organizational

All corporate governance documents (LLC Agreement, side letters [if any]) for the Company, and if applicable, its subsidiaries

Legal entity chart of the Company and its subsidiaries, if any

List of all managers, directors and officers of the Company

Minutes of meetings and actions of the Company's manager(s), director(s) or any committee thereof and the Company's security holders

Legal entity chart of the Company and its subsidiaries, if any

All corporate governance documents

List of all managers, directors and officers of the Company

Employment, consulting, severance or other similar agreements

Form of confidentiality, non-competition, non-solicitation and/or invention agreements for employees

All corporate policies, manuals and employee handbooks

Employee and independent contractor chart that includes the current salary/wage rate, exempt/non-exempt status, job function and part-time/full-time status

IT and Data

Description of the types of information collected and stored by the Company relating to its customers

Descriptions, summaries, complaints and other documents related to data privacy breaches or alleged breaches

Logs or summaries of all material complaints received by the Company regarding data privacy or data security in the past three years, as well as any unresolved complaints regardless of age

Indicate whether the Company undertook any policy or operational changes in connection with the California Consumer Privacy Act (CCPA)

Risk assessments and internal or external audit reports addressing the Company's privacy and data security controls

The Company's internal policies and procedures related to information security, including any policies addressing system/network security; data classification; data retention; data security breach incident response; access controls; and disaster recovery/business continuity

List of all domain names registered to or used by the Company

Identify all material third party software used by the Company

The Company's internal policies and procedures related to information security, including any policies addressing system/network security; data classification; data retention; data security breach incident response; access controls; and disaster recovery/business continuity

Risk assessments and internal or external audit reports addressing the Company's privacy and data security controls

Finances - Quality of Earnings

Description of any commitments, contingencies and guarantees

Detail of all A/R write-offs during Delivery Duty Paid; please identify when the original revenue was recorded

Detail of credits in A/R as of Year-end and Interim

Detailed analysis of key metrics used by Management for Delivery Duty Paid

Detailed listing of additions and disposals for Delivery Duty Paid

Detailed listing of cash disbursements (checks, wires, ACH, EFT, etc) for Delivery Duty Paid including date, vendor name, and amount

Detailed monthly WIP schedules for completed and in process projects throughout Delivery Duty Paid including total contract value, estimated costs, and estimated GM, costs incurred to date (Mat, Lab, & OH), revenues recognized to date, and billings to date

Bank reconciliations for all cash accounts for each month-end from January 2020 through January 2023

Capex budget for current and subsequent fiscal years

Contracts for top 5 customers

Copies of all employment and union agreements, if applicable

Copies of all facility and operating leases including the most recent future minimum payment schedules

Detailed support for prepaid assets (expenses and health insurance) as of Year-end and Interim

Detailed support for Service WIP as of Year-end and Interim

Provide commentary as to payment status of accounts aged greater than 90 days as of January 2023

General ledger transaction detail for Delivery Duty Paid

Finances - Tax

Contact information for and access to the internal personnel and external advisors responsible for all U.S. federal, state and local income and all other non-income (payroll, etc.) tax matters with respect to the Company

Copies of all federal, state, local, and foreign income and franchise tax returns filed for the Designated Timeframe

Copies of detailed trial balances (showing individual Company detail if consolidated) for the Designated Timeframe. (Tax only engagements)

Copies of financial statements for the Designated Timeframe with footnotes and any relevant supporting schedules. (Tax only engagements)

Details of any anticipated pre-transaction restructurings that will occur in connection with the proposed transaction. To the extent available, Provide any structuring decks, organizational structure charts, tax analysis, and/or valuations prepared in connection with the anticipated pre-transaction restructurings

Documents related to acquisition or merger activity in the past

Documents related to amended federal, state or local tax returns for the Designated Timeframe

Documents related to any nexus questionnaires

Documents related to any outstanding credit balances for an extended period of time or any material outstanding checks or any other abandoned items

Documents related to any US federal, state, and local tax audits

Documents related to changes to corporate structure during the Designated Timeframe

Documents related to entities related to the Company by common ownership

Finances - Tax, Continued

Documents related to payroll tax returns

Documents related to real property tax in the states where real property exists

Documents related to the Company's tax advisor(s)

Documents related to the Supreme Court's decision in South Dakota v. Wayfair

Documents related to the Company taking the position that it is not subject to income tax under P.L. 86-272 in any states

Documents related to uncertain or unusual tax positions

Documents related to unclaimed property reports with any jurisdictions

Explanation of policy for withholding income taxes on nonresident employees performing services in other jurisdictions

Including extensions, were any of the Company's federal, state, and local tax returns for the Designated Timeframe filed late? (income, franchise, gross receipts, payroll, sales and use, property tax)

Describe the Company's organizational and ownership structure. If available, Provide an organizational chart illustrating the ownership structure

List in which states and local jurisdictions the Company is currently filing tax returns noting the years filed and the type of tax

Provide a copy of any nexus analysis and/or ASC 740-10 (FIN 48) analysis reports

Provide a list of states where the Company is registered for sales and use tax purposes

Does the Company collect sales tax from customers in any state?

Provide a list of tax functions performed in-house v. the tax advisor or a third-party professional

Provide a listing of any state, local, or other incentives

Provide a schedule of payroll by state based on the location of the employees

Finances - Tax, Continued

Provide a schedule of property based on location of the property that includes personal property owned, real property owned, and total rent by state for both real and personal property

Provide a summary of closed, ongoing, and pending US federal, state, and local tax audits (e.g., income, payroll, sales and use, excise) for the past six years

Provide apportionment information for any flow-through entities that the Company owns or has owned in the Designated Timeframe. Explain how these factors were used in determining overall apportionment for the Company

Provide copies of all tax returns

Provide the articles of incorporation or organization

Provide the states where the Company's employee or independent contractors traveled during Designated Timeframe

Schedule indicating and explaining any changes in SUTA rates

Statement indicating state residency of all shareholders

Intellectual Property

Agreements relating to intellectual property rights, options to intellectual property rights, research and development, licenses, inventions or other interests in intellectual property

Agreements requiring or providing for the deposit into escrow or disclosure of the Company's source code or other technology

Agreements with independent contractors or consultants relating to the development of intellectual property owned or used by the Company

All license agreements (as licensor or licensee)

Any post-grant proceedings or other challenges of an issued patent or registered trademark before a US or foreign patent and trademark office

Intellectual Property, Continued

Correspondence or other documentation dealing with actual or alleged infringement of patents, trademarks, copyrights, trade secrets or other IP rights, including any "cease and desist" or "invitations to license" letters

Identify all material third party software used by the Company

Identify and describe any restrictions or limitations regarding the use, sale, distribution, commercialization or exploitation of any IP

List of all domain names registered to or used by the Company

List of all patents, trademarks, service marks, registered copyrights and other registered intellectual property ("IP") owned by the Company and applications and registrations for any of the foregoing types of IP

List of all proprietary software owned by the Company, indicating whether such software was developed by Company employees or contractors or acquired from a third party

All agreements with independent contractors or consultants relating to the development of intellectual property owned or used by the Company

Legal

Current reserves for litigation and other contingencies

Litigation files, including pleadings, for all existing matters

Provide any settlement agreements for the past three years

Provide copies of any outstanding judgments, decrees, injunctions, consents, orders, etc. requiring payment or limiting the business

Schedule of all threatened or pending litigation and investigations

List of all patents, trademarks, service marks, registered copyrights and other registered intellectual property ("IP") owned by the Company and applications and registrations for any of the foregoing types of IP

Appendix

Sample Earnout Language

This is an example of the language that may describe your earnout. Like the LOI, each commitment is different, but this should give you a sense for the type of language that's used.

Earnout

The Purchaser shall pay the Seller the following amounts in addition to the Closing Purchase Price:

For the 2022 Earnout Timeframe, if the 2022 Earnout EBITDA is less than $AMOUNT, the 2022 Earnout Payment shall be $0. If the 2022 Earnout EBITDA is equal to or more than $AMOUNT, the 2022 Earnout Payment shall be $AMOUNT.

For the 2023 Earnout Timeframe, if the 2023 Earnout EBITDA is less than $AMOUNT, the 2023 Earnout Payment shall be $0. If the 2023 Earnout EBITDA is equal to or more than $AMOUNT, the 2023 Earnout Payment shall be $AMOUNT.

"2022 Earnout Timeframe" and "2023 Earnout Timeframe" refer to the calendar year ended December 31, 2022 or December 31, 2023, respectively.

"2022 Earnout EBITDA" and "2023 Earnout EBITDA" refer to the consolidated net income of the Seller's sales team for the respective Earnout Periods, determined according to GAAP, as consistently applied. This calculation will exclude all extraordinary items of income, interest and investment income, and gains on any sale or similar transaction not in the ordinary course of business.

The Seller sales team, for the purposes of calculating the 2022 Earnout EBITDA and 2023 Earnout EBITDA, refers to the Seller's business as conducted by the employees of the Purchaser who are allocated to such sales team. To clarify, revenue (and related expense) will be allocated among Purchaser sales teams based on which sales team performs the applicable customer work, not which sales team sourced the customer.

The Purchaser is obligated to provide the Seller with monthly unaudited, consolidated financial statements of the Seller sales team within 15 days after the end of each month throughout the 2022 Earnout Timeframe and 2023 Earnout Timeframe.

These statements shall include operating income, net income, EBITDA, adjusted net income, and adjusted EBITDA, and each adjustment shall be specified in detail and accompanied by notes.

Within 30 days of receiving the Earnout Payment Notice, the Seller may dispute the statement and deliver a Disputed Earnout Payment Notice to the Purchaser stating the basis for their objection to the Applicable Earnout Payment and the proposed amount, including the disputed items. The Seller and the Purchaser will then attempt to reach an agreement on the Applicable Earnout Payment as soon as possible. If the Seller fails to deliver the Disputed Earnout Payment Notice or accepts the calculation of the Applicable Earnout Payment within the specified time, the Applicable Earnout Payment in the Earnout Payment Notice will be considered accurate and final.

If the Seller and the Purchaser cannot reach an agreement on the Applicable Earnout Payment within 30 days of the delivery of the Disputed Earnout Payment Notice, the Designated Arbitrator will be engaged to resolve the dispute. The Designated Arbitrator will only address the disputed items specified in the notice, and will select either the Seller's or the Purchaser's proposal, and then determine the Applicable Earnout Payment as modified only by the resolution of such items. The non-prevailing party shall bear the fees, costs, and expenses of the Designated Arbitrator. If there are multiple disputed items and a party prevailed on some but not all of them, then the non-prevailing party will be determined based on the difference between their non-prevailing and prevailing positions.

Within 30 days after the settlement of the Applicable Earnout Payment, the Purchaser shall pay the Applicable Earnout Payment to the Seller.

Thank You

The best parts of this book are the stories, and I didn't write them—I just listened and shared them. The people I interviewed deserve the credit for the ideas in those stories. Thank you to Maria Giudice from Hot Studio, Gavin Lew from User Centric, Christian Barnard from T3, Sue and Alan Cooper, Phil Barrett from Flow Interactive, Matthew Robinson from Idean, Crystal Rutland from Particle Design, Chris Conley from gravitytank, Max Burton from Matter, and Doreen Lorenzo from frog—thank you all for sharing your experiences in such detail and with such candor.

Thank you to all of the others I spoke with who were instrumental in shaping my understanding of the acquisition experience for design consultancies, particularly Theo Forbath, Nick Gould, Abby Godee, Kevin McDonald, and Collin Cole.

Thank you to John Cooper from 7 Mile Advisors, who was our M&A advisor during our company sale; to Julie Dale from Heyman & Associates, our CPA; and Brian Spross and Robyn Siers from Jones & Spross, our attorneys.

Thank you to Tiffany Braden, proofreader extraordinaire.

Thank you to Matt Franks and Chad Fisher, my partners at Modernist Studio, and to Chrissy Cowdrey and Swava Hooks, additional partners at my new studio, Narrative.

And endless thank yous and appreciations to my wife, Jess, who supported me through the entire sale process and has been my love and partner for 23 years and counting. Jess, I promise I won't say "EBITDA" any more at home :)

About the Author

Jon is a partner at Narrative, a design strategy consultancy. He is also a co-founder of Modernist Studio, which was acquired in 2021, and is the founder of the design school Austin Center for Design.

He was previously the Vice President of Design at Blackboard, the largest educational software company in the world. He joined Blackboard with the acquisition of MyEdu, a startup focused on helping students succeed in college and get jobs.

Jon has also held the positions of Executive Director of Design Strategy at Thinktiv, a venture accelerator in Austin, Texas, and both Principal Designer and Associate Creative Director at frog design, a global innovation firm. He has been a Professor of Interaction and Industrial Design at the Savannah College of Art and Design, where he was instrumental in building both the Interaction and Industrial Design undergraduate and graduate programs. Jon has also held the role of Director for the Interaction Design Association (IxDA), and Editor-in-Chief of *Interactions* magazine, published by the ACM. He has taught at the University of Texas at Austin, the Center for Design Studies of Monterrey, in Mexico, and Malmö University, in Sweden.

Jon is the author of a number of other books, including:

- Exposing the Magic of Design: A Practitioner's Guide to the Methods and Theory of Synthesis, published by Oxford University Press
- Creative Clarity, published by Brown Bear Press
- Well-Designed: How to Use Empathy to Create Products People Love, published by Harvard Business Review Press

Made in United States
North Haven, CT
15 July 2023